memories

memories

Elaine Paige

CELEBRATING 40 YEARS IN THE THEATRE

Foreword by

Andrew Lloyd Webber

OBERON BOOKS
LONDON

First published in 2008 by Oberon Books Ltd
521 Caledonian Road, London N7 9RH
tel 020 7607 3637 / fax 020 7607 3629
info@oberonbooks.com /
www.oberonbooks.com

A catalogue record for this book is available
from the British Library.

Front cover, back cover flap and chapter
photographs © Nobby Clark 2008

For other copyright information, see
Photograph Credits, p 160.

ISBN: 978-1-84002-852-2

Printed by Antony Rowe Ltd, Chippenham

THANKS TO:

Andrew Lloyd Webber,
Everyone at Oberon Books,
Kate Weston, Michael Storrs,
Malcolm Prince, Nobby Clark,
Pam Gems, Brian Sibley,
Don Black, Brook Land,
Diane Langton, Jonathan Bergman,
Paul Nicholas, Tim Rice
and Crewe Issue.

www.elainepaige.com

Contents

Foreword

PUT IT THIS WAY. The expletive Elaine Paige uttered on the stage of the Palace Theatre at the final Evita auditions back in the spring of 1978 would not have inspired Alfred Lord Tennyson to compose his opus to 'Elaine the fair'. But it did get the prodigiously talented Elaine the role of Eva Peron, the role she created in Hal Prince's legendary production of *Evita*, the musical written by Tim Rice and myself.

The endless auditions had got down to three girls. Hal finally left it to Tim and me to decide who was to play Eva. At the eleventh hour, after Elaine had done yet another brilliant audition of *Rainbow High*, the song that really sorts the Evas out, I was convinced that Elaine was our girl.

But it was such a momentous casting decision that Tim and I thought that for safety's sake we should hear Elaine sing *Don't Cry for Me Argentina* for the umpteenth time. That's when she uttered the words that clinched her the role.

We had to find a girl to play Evita who not only had a throat of concrete, but had a heart, and who was clearly more than capable of throwing a diva's tantrum. I called Hal. Elaine was cast.

Elaine, of course, went on to give one of the finest musical theatre performances of all time, and *Evita* was established all over the world.

I have known Elaine now for over 30 years. In that time she has been justly dubbed the first lady of British musical theatre. She rescued me when we lost Judi Dench as our leading lady in *Cats* after Judi's tragic accident.

But not only did Elaine step into the show at unbelievably short notice, she also premiered *Memory* which to date is the most successful song I have written.

She has a 'belt' voice in areas where no self-respecting angel will ever dare to tread and she has the heart to use this God-given voice in a way that imbues it with true emotion. That performance of *Memory* from *Cats* is testimony to her astonishing ability to tug at the heart strings.

There are many, me included, who believe her performance as Norma Desmond in my *Sunset Boulevard* to be up there with the very best. She has, of course, played many roles in musicals unconnected with me. I think of her extraordinary performance in *Piaf*, and the amazing quality she brought to Tim Rice's *Chess*.

So why is Elaine so special? Here's why:

I adore and admire her because she is a consummate professional. She has a burning desire to achieve what few others can even dare to aspire to. And also, she's a tiny bit like me.

She's naughty. Only her friends know what fun this outrageously talented girl can be. My life has been enriched both personally and musically by the wickedly contagious talent that is Elaine Paige.

ANDREW LLOYD WEBBER
London 2008

1
Beginnings

LOOKING AGAIN at pictures of myself back then with my classmates reminds me why I was so insecure. I'm short, plain, flat-chested with frizzy hair. Boys were never interested in me, because I still looked as if I was in primary school.

That 'schoolgirl' was born Elaine Jill Bickerstaff in Barnet, Hertfordshire, on the 5th March 1948, the second daughter of Irene Edith and Eric Edgar Bickerstaff.

Top left: Me, the new arrival, with my sister Marion, looking somewhat underwhelmed. I always wonder if she rather I'd had a proper job!

Top right: Presenting head mistress Miss Littlechild with a bouquet on her retirement, 1960. Looking every inch the primary school pupil – but actually twelve years old.

Above right: Southaw Secondary Modern Girl's School, Oakley Park. Class of '64. I'm third from left, front row.

Mum and Dad's wedding – 21st September 1940 – with both sets of grandparents. Left to right: Edgar James Martin Bickerstaff, Daisy May Hilda Johnson, Eric Edgar Bickerstaff, Irene Edith Bickerstaff (née Johnson), Edith Eliza Bickerstaff and Benjamin Drayson Johnson.

Music was in the family, passed down from my grandparents, who wrote and performed in concert parties. Although my father was an estate agent, music mattered most. He was the drummer in his four-piece band called The Arcadians. My mother was a milliner with her own shop. To this day I still can't pass a hat shop without trying on a few and, more often than not, coming out with at least one. Mum had a good singing voice. Her idols were Ella Fitzgerald and the crooners of the day, Perry Como, Andy Williams and Matt Monro. Dad's were Count Basie's big band, along with jazz drummers, Gene Krupa and Buddy Rich.

Below left: Dad on drums at a Christmas gig with Joe Passey on bass and the other members of The Arcadians.

Below right: Dad with his first drum kit.

Bottom: Mum's hat shop, Barnet.

Above: This snap shot of me was taken by Dad to record the momentous day when I first wore a leotard and ballet shoes. He was a keen photographer trying out his new Canon camera. It's clear for all to see that he hadn't yet fathomed the zoom lens.

Friday and Saturday nights were Dad's gig nights. In all weathers he loaded his drums into the car and with his war-time pal, Joe Passey, set off into the dark – a man driven! London winters in the Fifties were foggy. Real pea-soupers! You couldn't see your own hand in front of your face. But that never stopped Dad. Joe drove at a snail's pace, while Dad walked in front with a torch. Mum and I stood in the doorway watching them disappear. 'Madness!' she'd say, and then worry about him all night. What did *we* do? Go straight to the radiogram, open the lid, take out the LPs and listen to volumes 1 to 5 of Ella Fitzgerald.

The first record I ever bought was for my mother: Perry Como singing *Magic Moments*. We were big fans of the Perry Como and Andy Williams TV shows. The other show we loved was *Come Dancing*. I'd spend hours in our front room singing and dancing, pretending I was either Ella Fitzgerald or Ginger Rogers wearing a sequinned 'ballroom dress'.

In Barnet High street, above Burton's men's outfitters, was Stanley Jackson's North Twenty Dance Studio, buzzing with other *Come Dancing* fans. My great ambition was to follow in my cousin Carolyn's footsteps and join the formation team, until I went to Southaw Secondary Modern Girl's school in Oakley Park.

Ann Hill was head of the music department. It was she who first recognised my passion for music and encouraged me to sing. In fact, she introduced us all to the glories of Handel and Mozart, teaching us music theory. The culminating achievement was an end of term performance of the *Messiah*.

Right: With Ann Hill, head of music, Southaw Secondary Modern Girl's School, after my concert at the Lyceum Theatre, London, 2006.

We also staged *The Boy Mozart*, an operetta based on the composer's life and work. I sang the mezzo role, Bastienne, from the
opera *Bastien and Bastienne*, the first of many emotional songs
which have shaped my career. When I sobbed at the end of the
aria the audience gasped. They thought the poor child had dried!
Didn't they know I was acting? My father did, though, and duly
asked 'Would you like to go to drama school?'
A dream come true! I could hardly believe it.
In suburbia we didn't do things like that, but
Dad must have wanted me to have the chance
in life he didn't have. The war got in the way of
so many people's lives. By the end of the year
I'd enrolled at the Aida Foster Stage School,
Golders Green, for a three-year student drama
course. I don't know who was more excited – me
or my parents.

*Above: As Bastienne in the school
production of* The Boy Mozart.
*Ann Hill conducting, me on her right in
an orange frock.*

*Below: First portrait at the Aida Foster
Stage School aged 16.*

Below: Composite of ten-by-eights for the Aida Foster Stage School. A little make-up and I'm growing up!

The Aida Foster stage school also ran an agency. Each student was required to have on file a selection of ten-by-eights to demonstrate versatility. I did my best to look like Brigitte Bardot, though I *still* looked wide-eyed and innocent. But at sixteen, with a bit of make up and a flick-up Fifties hairstyle, I managed the leap from plain Jane to wannabe Doris Day!

AIDA FOSTER AGENCY
SPE 1178

ELAINE PAIGE

LSO-1109 STEREO

THE ORIGINAL BROADWAY CAST RECORDING

DAVID MERRICK
IN ASSOCIATION WITH
BERNARD DELFONT
PRESENTS

ANTHONY NEWLEY

CYRIL RITCHARD

IN THE NEW
LESLIE BRICUSSE – ANTHONY NEWLEY
MUSICAL

THE ROAR OF THE GREASEPAINT
– THE SMELL OF THE CROWD

RCA VICTOR
DYNAGROOVE
RECORDING

Left: I bought this original LP of the Broadway cast recording of The Roar of the Greasepaint… *as a memento of my first musical. For me Broadway was years away.*

My first audition came in 1964. It was for the national tour of the new Leslie Bricusse/Anthony Newley musical, *The Roar of the Greasepaint – the Smell of the Crowd*, starring Norman Wisdom. For my audition I sang *I'm Just a Girl Who Cain't Say No* from *Oklahoma*, and it was the first time I was to hear the dismissive 'Thank you!'

Yet Aida Foster was convinced I was right for the show, and suggested I went back under another name. I thought she was mad. 'Wouldn't they recognise me?' How naive! I got the part, a Chinese urchin, and kept the name – Elaine Paige.

So where did my new name come from? Because I needed it in such a hurry, I was reduced to flicking through the family phone book on the hall table, hoping that a name would somehow jump off the page… 'Ah, "page"!' I thought – then, 'Better still, why not "Paige" with an "i"?'

Below: My first professional engagement. Elaine Bickerstaff becomes Elaine Paige.

The show didn't make it to the West End, although later it became a hit on Broadway – needless to say without any of us. The dreaded notice went up, the show closed, and I cried. Would I ever work again? Yes – as, guess what? Another urchin! Looking so young for my age (sixteen), along with my pal Wendy Padbury, I didn't need a costly chaperone, as required by law for child actors, so I cornered the market in urchins. For six months, working on the classic film version of Lionel Bart's *Oliver!* I got up at four a.m. and would collect Leila Hart, a singer on the production, and we'd drive to Shepperton Studios in

my little Standard 10, which cost me £60 second-hand. In fact, I peaked as an urchin in *Oliver!* If you don't blink, you can see me wearing a long wig next to Oliver and the Artful Dodger at the end of the rousing *Consider Yourself*, and as a dancing housemaid during the haunting song, *Who Will Buy?* I'm the one on the right hand edge of the frame.

Of course, in truth, I wanted to play the role of Nancy so that I could sing the supremely devotional *As Long as He Needs Me*. Another besotted female in love with a lousy no-good villain, yet is this not one of the most powerful love songs of all time?

Below: On the rehearsal set of the film Oliver! *I'm the moody-looking girl peering over the man's shoulder in front of the ladder, with my friend Helen Worth (now Gail Platt in* Coronation Street*) standing next to me. The film's director, Sir Carol Reed, is at the extreme right of the picture, hands in pockets, wearing sunglasses.*

*My Mum and Dad's Sixtieth Wedding Anniversary celebration in
2000. My sister Marion and I have always enjoyed organising parties
for family birthdays and anniversaries. Here with her daughters Sophie
(second from left) and Joanna (right) and husband Richard. A small
but happy bunch.*

Above: My last night party of Chess *in 1986 (see Chapter 6) at
L'Escargot restaurant. Left to right: front row, Richard, Mum, Dad
and Sophie; back row, Betty Winter (family friend), cousin Carolyn,
Joanna, cousin Laurence and Marion.*

At the Louvre in Paris 1995 with Dad, Marion, Mum, Richard.
We enjoyed many jaunts together over the years. Paris had become
so important to me after I went to research the role of Piaf.
(See Chapter 7.)

On the steps of Buckingham Palace after my OBE investiture in 1995,
before meeting up with close friends and family for a slap-up lunch.
What a proud day!

2

Hair

Book and Lyrics: Gerome Ragni and James Rado

Music: Galt MacDermot

Shaftesbury Theatre, London, 1968

Maybe That's Your Problem

Book: Lionel Chetwynd

Lyrics: Don Black

Music: Walter Schars

Roundhouse, London, 1971

Rock Carmen

Book and Lyrics: Herb Hendler

Music: Michael Hughes

Roundhouse, London, 1972

Hair

HAIR WAS a radical show for its time. It was written by two out-of-work actors, Gerome Ragni and James Rado, with music by Galt MacDermot. A psychedelic milestone of the Sixties, it tackled the Vietnam war head on. This was the first protest musical. The cast were racially integrated teenagers with a conscience, and with its famous nude scene, it could never have been done in Britain if, on the eve of the first performance, Parliament hadn't changed the law on theatre censorship after more than 200 years.

In 1968 I joined the cast at the Shaftesbury Theatre a week after one of the 'tribe', as the chorus was known, departed. It was my West End debut after eight auditions! The problem was I looked too neat and tidy and they wanted scruffy. I don't do scruffy. But I did try. I distressed my jeans by rolling them in the dirt in the garden and, to my mother's horror, wore an unironed T-shirt, and I still didn't get the job! But Cindy Ann Lee dropped out and suddenly I was in.

Hair got mixed reviews, but there was a surprising endorsement from Irving Wardle, veteran drama critic of *The Times*: 'Nothing else remotely like it has yet struck the West End. Its

Right: With my pals from Hair, *Liz White (middle) and Diane Langton (bottom).*

honesty and passion give it the quality of a true theatrical cele-bration – the joyous sound of a group of people telling the world exactly what they feel.'

As well as being in the tribe, I understudied Annabel Leventon in the role of Sheila. It was the first time I sang solo on stage. The song was *Easy to be Hard*, a soulful ballad which expressed the angst of youth at the time: war, social injustice, the bomb. A time of great change. The class system was breaking down – hippy flower-power, rebelling against the establishment, equal rights for women, sexual freedom. We all thought we were going to change the world. Free love was rampant and so were we.

Art in all its forms blossomed. London was the centre of advances in music, theatre, fashion, pop art, drugs and rock'n'roll. The Swinging Sixties had arrived. I was there, and I remember it! *Hair* was the show to be seen and to be seen at. They all came, even royalty. Princess Anne danced on stage with other audience members and the cast. Unheard of! It was the beginning of a new era of freedom of expression. But all this optimism did not alter the fact that 'LBJ' and 'Tricky Dicky', as the show proclaimed, were waging a fruitless war in Vietnam, where so many American soldiers were losing their lives, also in the name of freedom. Forty years on, the world turns and nothing much has changed.

Below: The original London cast of Hair, *1968. I'm second row, second smiling face from the left. Front row (left to right): Linda Kendrick, Liz White, Paul Nicholas, Lucy Fenwick, Kookie Eaton, and Sonja Kristina. Second row (left to right): Peter Oliver, Tim Curry (behind me), Linbert Spencer (half a face), J Vincent (Vince) Edward, Ena Cabayo, and Ethel Coley. Back row (left to right): Gary Hamilton, Peter Straker, Annabel Leventon and Oliver Tobias. A happy hippy bunch. All except Linda Kendrick (bottom left), who'd had a row with her boyfriend. I'm behind Paul Nicholas, whom I would work with many more times to come.*

Maybe That's Your Problem

A show about premature ejaculation! Why write a musical about it? You may well ask. All I can say is that the 'problem' was revealed in the first scene. I was in the chorus again. It was the first time I worked with lyricist Don Black. One song that he particularly liked was called *A Night to Remember*. For what, I wonder?! The show closed after only 18 performances. The lyricist Alan Jay Lerner told Don the show should have been called *Shortcomings!* It was one of two musicals I was in at The Roundhouse, Chalk Farm. The other was *Rock Carmen*.

Right: with Don Black, lyricist of Maybe That's your Problem, *in 1987.*

Below: The cover of the score of Maybe That's Your Problem.

Rock Carmen

Hair brought us the rock musical – *Jesus Christ Superstar* and *Godspell* among them. *Rock Carmen* was, of course, a rock version of Bizet's opera, in which I played Michaela (renamed Michelle), the nice girl who Don José leaves for Carmen, the temptress. As in the opera, Michaela / Michelle gets one of the best numbers. In the rock version it's called *Do What You Want with Me*, a ballad about love lost and a broken heart. There would be many such songs to come. But this one was special. Michelle was my first leading role in a new work.

The rock musical ushered in a new era of shows for a new beat generation. Until then the musical was dominated by a handful of great Broadway composers – George Gershwin, Cole Porter, Jerome Kern, Rodgers and Hart, Rodgers and Hammerstein, Lerner and Loewe. *West Side Story* by Leonard Bernstein and Stephen Sondheim was a big influence on me as a schoolgirl. I wanted to play the role of Maria from the moment I heard it on record.

In Britain, Noël Coward and Lionel Bart had been holding the fort with successes like *Sail Away* and *Oliver!* It wasn't until Andrew Lloyd Webber and Tim Rice came along that British musicals achieved phenomenal international success. But theirs was a different approach. In the earlier musicals the show always came first and the recordings and hit songs followed. But with Andrew and Tim, the recordings came first, promoting the shows before they had ever been seen. A canny marketing strategy? No, I believe by happy accident, but nevertheless it was to change the face of musical theatre forever. Globalisation! *Joseph and the Amazing Technicolor Dreamcoat*, *Jesus Christ Superstar*, *Evita*, *Cats*, *Chess* and *Phantom of the Opera* among others ushered in a rich harvest of the all-British musical, and it was my good fortune to be involved from the start.

3

Jesus Christ Superstar

Lyrics: Tim Rice

Music: Andrew Lloyd Webber

Palace Theatre, London, 1972

Nuts

Devised and directed by Joan Littlewood

Theatre Royal, Stratford East, 1973

Grease

Music, Book and Lyrics: Jim Jacobs and Warren Casey

New London Theatre, 1973

Billy

Book: Dick Clement and Ian La Frenais

Lyrics: Don Black

Music: John Barry

Theatre Royal, Drury Lane, 1974

The Boyfriend

Music, book and lyrics: Sandy Wilson

Haymarket Theatre, Leicester, 1976

Jesus Christ Superstar

A modern 'opera', sung-through without spoken dialogue, based on the last days in the life of Christ, ending with the crucifixion. Who would have thought the show-going public would take to it? The church condemned the show for sensationalising the central story in the Gospels with loud rock music and hip, streetwise language. The critics also condemned it. But the public already knew the music from the album, which had been on general release for some time. I first heard the title track on a demo recording of the original concept album. Murray Head, who was singing the role of Judas, played it to me himself in the wardrobe department (there was no green room) of the Shaftesbury theatre while we were both in *Hair*.

I couldn't audition for the original *JCS* company at the Palace Theatre as I was already committed to *Rock Carmen*. When Diane Langton, my pal from *Hair* days, rang me to say she wanted to leave, I got my chance. It was the first of many auditions I would

undergo at this theatre, one of which would much later alter the course of my life. The producers insisted that she would have to help them recast. I auditioned and got into the chorus and I was given a tiny part as one of the three Hosannah Angels, a featured moment as a Supremes-style backing group for *Simon Zealotes*. They also wanted me to understudy the role of Mary Magdalene. As much as I loved her song *I Don't Know How to Love Him*, I knew that my understudying days must end if I was ever to be taken seriously as a lead actor. So I turned down that part of the job. It would be some time later that I would record the song on my album, *Stages*.

I still feel nostalgic about that year of carefree nights playing in the chorus of *JCS*. Half the cast were stoned half of the time, which added to the fun. As well as playing an Hosannah Angel, I was a leper! Victor Spinetti was a wonderfully charismatic Herod, and I had the honour of lying on his bed in his harem! Paul Nicholas was the best Jesus of them all. That voice! I've never heard *Gethsemane* better sung. He was also Claude in *Hair*, so we already knew each other. In fact, there was a great sense of belonging among the casts of these shows. Long-lasting friendships were born. We were like an itinerant 'family', going from musical to musical in the West End.

Above: Paul Nicholas in Jesus Christ Superstar.

Nuts

Nuts was a truly anarchic revue, a rag-bag of playlets, sketches and songs. In a nutshell, a crazy show. It was devised and directed by the legendary Joan Littlewood for Theatre Workshop, which Joan ran with Gerry Raffles at the Theatre Royal Stratford East. Joan was a great teacher, but I was terrified of her. She could be a fierce critic and make everybody cry. 'Don't fold your arms like that! Your body language is saying "Don't come near me! Don't come near me!" You've got to loosen up!' she said. Ever compelling us to be imaginative and spontaneous, her goal was for you to lose your inhibitions and let go of propriety. So that's what we did during the Jeanette MacDonald–Nelson Eddy spoof duet *When I'm Calling You*. I'm singing the verse in a prim soprano stance, wearing a beautiful ball gown; and, unbeknown to the audience, 'Nelson Eddy' comes up from the trapdoor, lifts the hem of my skirt and delivers a pint of milk! He then strolls on dressed as the milkman to finish the duet.

Any mishaps on stage would be used in performance. So if a door handle came off in your hand, you had to do something with it. Indeed, whatever happened on stage had value when you worked with Joan. The watchword in this show was spontaneity! Repetition was duly frowned on. Above all, surprise your audience. Never do anything the same way twice. So I was expected to make entrances and exits from a different point every night, even from the audience. If I'd flown down from the balcony she would have loved it. Indeed, one of my numbers was a riot. While I was singing *Summertime* from Gershwin's *Porgy and Bess*, at the moment I got to the line 'fish are jumping' fresh wet cod were flung at me from the wings. Whack! Whack! I kept going and threw the fish back into the wings, but then anarchy finally took over. Not caring if I was adding injury to insult, I started hurling the fish at the audience. Mayhem ensued. But I made it that night in Joan's eyes and she gave me a kiss and a big hug. Phew!

Grease

A new phase in my career begins when I take over the leading role of Sandy Dumbrowski, the Sandra Dee 'nice girl next door' character in the fifties-style musical, *Grease*. What's more, I was co-starring with my old pal, Paul Nicholas. We both left *Jesus Christ Superstar* at the same time to jive our way into 'Rydell High School', missing the chance though, to star opposite Richard Gere who Paul was replacing. I replaced Stacey Gregg.

Grease looks back at the pop culture of the Fifties – beehive hair-dos, hula hoop skirts, jeans and leather jackets. It was my first leading role in the West End. For once, it's actually the girl who gets the guy, but the main appeal was the transformation from sweet girl Sandy to Sandy the rocker, dressed from head to toe in black leather. The final number is a raunchy duet, Paul Nicholas and me jiving our way through *We Go Together*.

Me (centre) as Sandy Dumbrowski in Grease, *the oh-so-sweet 'Sandra D' girl-next-door who later rocks it up.*

Above: With Paul Nicholas in We Go Together, *the last number in the show.*

This was an energetic musical, too energetic one night for the new understudy who had to go on as Rizzo and do a heavy jive number, in which Paul Nicholas twirls her round at high speed in a twist lift. No one had told the poor girl to pin her wig on. A lacquered beehive flew off into the orchestra and miraculously ended up on a drumstick. You couldn't have done it if you rehearsed it a thousand times. Nonplussed, the drummer put the wig on! I was hidden behind a scrim waiting for my next scene. I watched the understudy run off in tears. By now I was also in tears – tears of laughter – and still laughing uncontrollably when the scrim rose. Fortunately, the audience thought I was in a state of deep emotion as I began to sing *It's Raining on Prom Night.*

Grease has since become one of the most successful musicals of all time. The music suited me well. Like everyone else in my generation, I grew up listening to Dusty Springfield, Brenda Lee, Dionne Warwick, Cilla Black, Lulu and the Supremes. The guys were Elvis, Cliff Richard, Buddy Holly, Marty Wilde, Billy Fury, the Beach Boys, Ricky Nelson, and the Everly Brothers. I knew all their songs. The Everlys' big hits, *Cathy's Clown* and *All I Have to Do Is Dream,* I sang in close harmony with my childhood chum, Heather Gibbins, who lived across the road.

Right: Jiving with Paul in rehearsals.

Billy

The musical, *Billy*, is based on *Billy Liar*, the novel by Keith Waterhouse. This had already been a successful stage play, starring Albert Finney, and an even more successful film with Tom Courtenay. There was also a TV sitcom with Jeff Rawle. In this musical version the working-class Yorkshire lad, Billy Fisher, a Walter Mitty fantasist, was played by Michael Crawford. Michael was at the peak of his TV stardom as Frank Spencer in the sitcom *Some Mothers Do 'Ave 'Em*. So *Billy* was tipped to be a hit. I created the role of Rita, a brassy, no-nonsense girlfriend (played by Gwendolyn Watts in the film). Rita was a loudmouth, and I discovered I had the voice to match, able to sing *Any Minute Now* without a microphone. To balance the sound, however, the newly invented body mike was used by all of us.

Many stories have been told about how 'difficult' Michael could be. There were tears and walk-outs. Michael's understudy, Billy Boyle, a hot-tempered Irishman, got so incensed in rehearsal he grabbed Michael by the throat. Peter Bowles left the show because he didn't want to be 'directed' by Michael as well as Patrick Garland. No actor can work with two directors at the same time.

As Rita with two-timing Billy (Michael Crawford): You Dirty Rotten Scoundrel.

Part of the problem was that Michael was a dedicated perfectionist, a hard worker, ever demanding of himself and others. *Billy* was an enormous role, and the responsibility on Michael was huge, something I didn't really appreciate at the time. But I understood later when I began playing major roles myself. Above all, Michael was a great natural comedian. I often stood in the wings to watch him wield his magic, how he would get laughs with his daring, long pauses and brilliant comic timing. A superb clown!

Below: With Gay Soper and Michael Crawford, in one of Billy's many fantasies – Ambrosia.

I shared a dressing room with Billy's other girlfriends, played by Gay Soper and Diana Quick. Diana wasn't in Act One, so she spent her time in the dressing room doing marvellous things like writing novels and restringing wicker chairs! Gay was a great morale booster and a lot of fun and remains a good friend. Other terrific members of the cast included Avis Bunnage, Bryan Pringle, Betty Turner, Billy Boyle and Barry James. Barry would tease me in the wings before I went on. One night I dried and invented an entirely new verse. Somehow it rhymed!

Billy was a triumph! 'The most successful British musical since *Oliver!*' said the *Daily Express*.

Above: You've gotta get a look! Here I am as Rita, strutting her stuff in a red satin mini skirt, and the highest platform boots I could get, giving me extra 'Eh-yup-chuck' clout.

Left: Gay Soper, Diana Quick and me as Billy's three girlfriends.

Below: Billy's parents and grandmother. Left to right: Betty Turner, Avis Bunnage and Bryan Pringle.

Right: A signed copy of the original London cast album which Michael Crawford signed for Mum using her nickname Dooker – nobody ever called her by her real name Irene. When she was a child in a pram everyone chucked her under the chin and said 'dooker, dooker, dooker' and the name stuck.

Below and opposite: There were some great publicity photos of Michael Crawford and me clowning around outside the stage door of the Palace Theatre, Manchester where the show tried out before coming into the West End. The shot of me running down the street with such a big TV star gave a boost to my career.

My thighs have never looked so good!

The Boyfriend

At the end of an eighteen-month run in *Billy* I was looking for something different. A good, solid drama, without a note of music, would broaden my range as a straight actress. Ho hum! Another musical it was. I took the role of Madcap Maisie in Leicester Haymarket Theatre's revival of Sandy Wilson's classic 'Roaring Twenties' musical, *The Boyfriend*. I made some lifelong friends in this production – Susie Wallace and Belinda Lang. We've travelled the length and breadth of the country in support of each other. The carrot of playing in a musical in Leicester was the promise of the role of Jackie Coryton in Noël Coward's *Hay Fever*, but then in comes an offer I can't refuse: Noël Coward will have to wait. I had a mortgage now.

Initially, the job was a sixteen-week contract in *One More Time*, a show for BBC TV Manchester. The show was produced by *Top of the Pops* producer, Johnny Stewart. The choreographer was Nigel Lythgoe, now internationally known as the producer of the TV talent shows *American Idol* and *So You Think You Can Dance*. It was a segued song show: eight singers peforming half an hour of back-to-back numbers, everything from barber shop to jazz, standards to the chart hits of the day. It was low budget and 'live' – in the sense that it was recorded in a single take. The pressure was enormous. If you screwed up your number, everyone else in the show had to record the whole thing again. On the odd occasion this occurred, one of the gang, John Christie, and I would walk off to the back of the set and try to lighten the situation by

Right: The Boyfriend: *being carried by (left to right) Jim Hooper, Crispin Thomas, David Timson and Martin Smith.*

Below: The MD and cast of the BBC TV series One More Time.

telling Dame Edna Everage jokes and Peter Cook and Dudley Moore stories. It was like being in weekly rep, learning new songs for every show. The low budget meant that we supplied our own costume materials. I scoured Shepherd's Bush market every week in search of them for the wardrobe department, who would make them up. The ratings went through the roof, cab drivers recognised me and I got my first fan letter!

Above and left: Won't You Charleston with Me? *with the wonderful Martin Smith, who died far too young.*

4

Evita

Lyrics: Tim Rice

Music: Andrew Lloyd Webber

Prince Edward Theatre, London, 1978

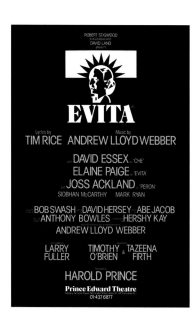

THE ROLE of Eva Peron has all the ingredients of tragic opera. Like Tosca and Violetta in *La Traviata*, Eva rose to fame and died a tragic, premature death. She came from the village of Los Toldos, Argentina – a fragile, tiny woman – and from these humble origins she clawed her way to the top, first becoming a small-time actress and eventually wife of the Argentinian President, Juan Peron. A beautiful gold digger, manipulative and socially ambitious, she remained ever loyal to the poor, 'the shirtless ones'. She was worshipped by them. She had the common touch and set up the Eva Peron Foundation for her charity work. None of this made her popular with the Argentinian oligarchy. She died of cancer at the age of 33.

Politics, passion and glamour – no wonder the story inspired one of the most popular musicals of all time. The extraordinary *Don't Cry for Me Argentina* is much more than a hit song. It is a key part of the plot. It provides one of the most dramatic scenes in the show: on the balcony of the Pink Palace in Buenos Aires, Eva appeals to the 'shirtless ones' to believe in her and her husband's political vision of Argentina. During rehearsals the great American impresario and director, Hal Prince, urged me to think of the song not only as a great tune, but also as a major political speech. 'Be forceful. Strong. Look the audience in the eye and make your point.' I follow his advice to this very day every time I sing it.

Getting the part was like running a marathon. If my then agent, Libby Glen, hadn't been so insistent at the time, I might never have got this magnificent role at all. I was already working. I had a small part in a film *The One and Only Phyllis Dixey*. I was in my 'serious actress' mode again, working with respected actors like Lesley-Anne Down and Patricia Hodge. While I was filming at the end of the North Pier, Blackpool, Libby contacted me and convinced me to buy the recording of *Evita* – the *White Album*, as it was known. I was perfect, she said, for role of Evita. Julie Covington, who sang Eva on the album, had decided not to play her on stage. So there was much press speculation about who would get the coveted role.

I bought the album on 17th February, 1977, and from the very first hearing I knew I had to play her.

I became obsessed with the Eva Peron story, the lyrics, the dazzling music, sung-through like *Jesus Christ Superstar* before it. Alas, the first round of auditions came and went. I got the flu! But on 9th March 1978 I auditioned at Drury Lane. I sang *On a Wonderful Day Like Today* from *The Roar of the Greasepaint – the Smell of the Crowd*, and the Beatles hit, *Yesterday*. The Beatles number I sang not as a pop song, but as a drama with a beginning, middle and end. My second audition was on the following day at the Palace Theatre. So began a series of six further auditions of increasing intensity, until one night my agent Libby arrived at

my flat, unannounced. It was midnight. She stood there regally, wearing a green cape, and in her slow Canadian drawl started to speak solemnly with gravitas:

'Elaine. Ah…have…come…t'tell…yoo…'
'What are you doing here?' I said.
'Elaine. Ah…have…come…t'tell…'
'Yes, Libby! What is it? Good news or bad news?'

But she was savouring the moment and started all over again!

'Ah…have…come…t'tell…yoo…'
'Yes! Yes! What?!'
'…that…the…pard…'
'Yes?!'
'…the…pard…of…Eva-a-a   Perrone…Evida!…the… most…coverded…role…in…'
'Oh, get on with it, Libby!'
'Liza Minnelli! Shirlee Maclaine! Barbra Streisssand! Petula Cla-a-rk! Ann-Ma-a-rgret! Faye Du-u-naway!… even Ra-a-quel…! izzz!…t' be…played!…bah…!'
'Libby!'

Then with a grand flourish of her cape she reveals a magnum of Dom Perignon.

'…the…pardiz…YOURS!'

Amazed, I screamed at the top of my voice. I couldn't believe it! The news that would change my life forever. The title role in a new Andrew Lloyd Webber and Tim Rice musical! What a shock! Thank heavens Eva Peron was only 5'2"!

In musical terms, however, I had come full circle from Mozart opera at school to singing this operatic role in *Evita*.

Below: My first press conference at the Robert Stigwood Organisation offices in Brook Street, London, announcing that I was to play Eva Peron in Evita. *I didn't know what was about to hit me.*

A few major musicals are now performed in Opera Houses throughout the world, and the list is growing. *Porgy and Bess* by George Gershwin is probably the first big Broadway musical to be regarded as an opera. More recently, *Sweeney Todd*, by Stephen Sondheim, was peformed at the Royal Opera House, Covent Garden. *Lost in the Stars* by Kurt Weill has been produced at Pittsburgh Opera. Who knows when *Evita* might become as much a part of the operatic repertory as *Tosca* and *Madam Butterfly*?

Above: The great Hal Prince directing me during rehearsals of Evita. *He told me to look the audience in the eyes – pick them out – during the speech that is* Don't Cry for Me Argentina*!*

Below: A young EP – that's Elaine Paige, not Eva Peron quite yet.

With Hal Prince, Tim Rice and Andrew Lloyd Webber. A publicity shot taken during rehearsal – Hal hated interruptions of his rehearsals!

THE SUNDAY TIMES *magazine*

JUNE 11, 1978

50 PESOS **CORREOS**

ELAINE PAIGE

ARGENTINA

THE NEW IMAGE OF EVITA

Left: June 11th 1978, just over a week before the opening of Evita. *I appeared on the cover of* The Sunday Times Magazine. *Here I am as Eva Peron on an Argentine postage stamp. The photo of my profile on which the illustration was based was taken before Eva's hair and make up had been designed. Already burying myself in the character of Eva, I came up with the 'look' – shame I didn't don a bigger pair of earrings!*

Right: So much press attention had been given to the show that, on the day it opened, 21st June 1978, all the newspaper advertisements had to do was show a picture of David Essex (playing Che Guevara), Joss Ackland (as Peron) and yours truly with the two words: Tonight… EVITA.

Tonight…EVITA

Above: The run up to Evita *was sheer media madness. On the morning of the first performance, the* Daily Mail *snapped me going into the stage door of the Prince Edward Theatre in Frith Street. I can't believe how relaxed I look – as if I hadn't a care in the world! But the truth was that I'd been totally focused on getting to grips with the role of Eva and really hadn't had time to come to terms with the full weight of responsibility that was about to descend on me. I had longed for an opportunity like this and, on that day, I simply couldn't wait to prove myself.*

Left: Having another fitting for the famous ball-gown – as long as I don't have to sew all the sequins on myself!

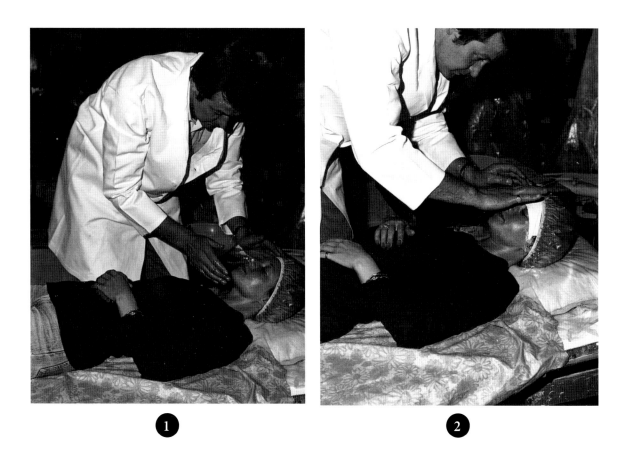

1

2

3

4

This page and opposite: Before playing Evita I had to get really plastered! Yes, Madame Tussaud's famous waxworks in London made a face-cast for the opening scene, where Eva's dead body is laid out in the coffin. I had to lie perfectly still while they smothered me in plaster of Paris and waited till it had set. An unforgettable but rather claustrophobic experience.

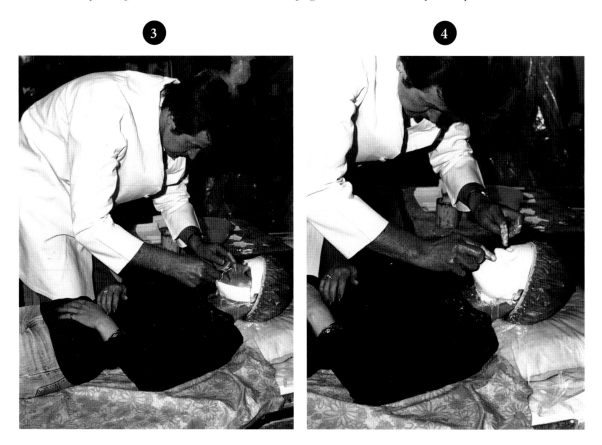

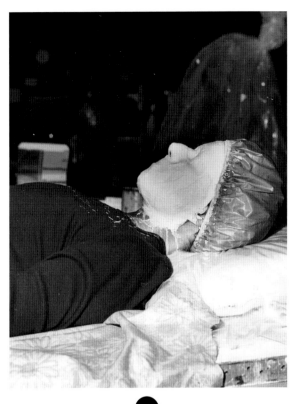

5

6

7

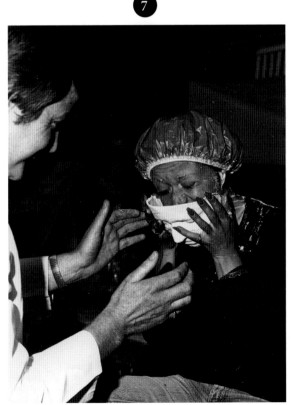

8

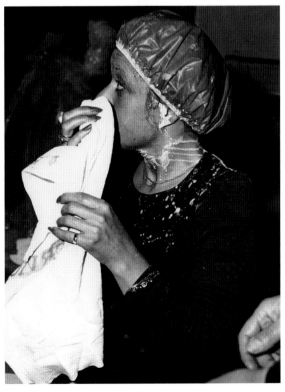

Above: Eva – with ambitions of bigger things.

Above: Dancing in Buenos Aires.

Above: Eva with her eye on Juan Peron.

Left: David was rather reserved, like his role in the show – standing outside the action and commenting on Eva's rise to power.

Joss, a brilliant Peron, was also a simply wonderful father figure throughout the rigorous rehearsal period, and nightly during performances – always encouraging and supportive.

Above: What no one knew was the nightly struggle I went through in order to perform Don't Cry for Me Argentina. *The only way up onto the balcony was by a vertical ladder at the back of the set and climbing it while wearing a voluminous gown would have been impossible without the help of a stagehand. Forget elegance or modesty: every show that guy was on the ladder just below me – underneath my skirts – holding the dress up until I reached the comparative safety of the platform! Where is that man today?!*

Right: Eva realises she is ill but won't give in to it. She wants to become Vice President.

Above: I played Eva from a young girl through to the sick, dying woman who had to be supported at the microphone as she made her last speech to her people.

Below: As Eva lies dying, she contemplates her life. 'Oh my daughter, oh my son, Understand what I have done.'

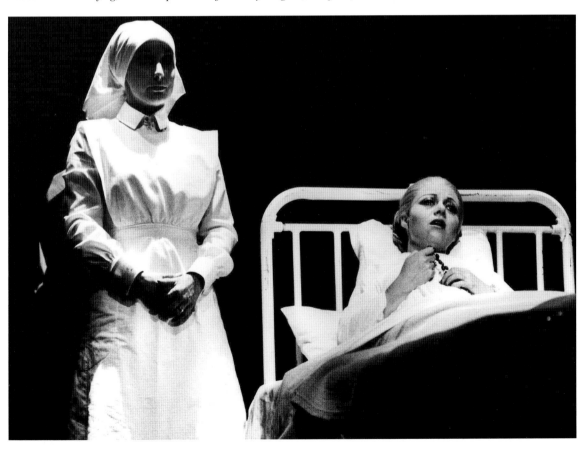

Above: Andrew Lloyd Webber's first night gift to me for Evita *– to win, you needed three Evas, not three lemons!*

Right: With my darling parents onboard SS Tattershall Castle, for the First Night Party. Life changed that night. 21st June 1978.

ELAINE PAIGE

THE TIMES JUNE 22 1978

A Puccini heroine captivated by her own dream

Irving Wardle

Elaine Paige's transformation in the role is one of the rewards of the evening: starting as a dumpy, mouse-haired little scold, acquiring the sumptuously voluptuous looks of a pampered courtesan, and taking on angular ascetic simplicity in her last phase. She handles the changes from public to private manner with shocking immediacy, and her voice fills the theatre like a whole brass section; most impressive of all, is the extent to which the shows Evita becoming totally captivated by her own dream.

Evening Standard:

MILTON SHULMAN

Elaine Paige successfully conveys the stocky pugnacious, magnetic charisma that Eva must have had and she handles her many singing chores with splendid authority.

Don't cry for Elaine, she's an instant superstar

A PINT-SIZED girl from Bognor Regis stepped over the brink of stardom last night and ran away with a show calling Evita at the Prince Edward Theatre, London.

Thirty-year-old Elaine Paige — the unknown actress who landed the part after a dozen top names were tipped for it — turned the much-ballyhooed new musical into a Cinderella story of her own.

Superstar is born . . . triumphant Elaine Paige

EVENING STANDARD, TUESDAY, JUNE 13, 1978—3

Daily Mail, Monday, December 4, 1978

Double triumph for Evita

Awards for Elaine and her show

By PAUL DONOVAN

THE sell-out musical Evita scored a double hit last night.

It was voted best musical in the Society of West End Theatre awards—and its star, Elaine Paige, took the award for best performance in a musical.

Singer Liza Minnelli presented an engraved urn to Tim Rice and Andrew Lloyd-Webber who wrote the show.

Two other new shows took major awards at the presentations, in the Cafe Royal in London's West End, which will be shown on BBC-TV's Nationwide tonight.

Tom Conti was voted actor of the year in a new play for his performance in Whose Life is it Anyway?

The show, which deals with mercy killing, was voted play of the year and playwright John Mortimer presented the prize to author Brian Clark.

The comedy of the year was Filumena and actress Joan Plowright—who co-stars in it

Turn to Page 2, Col. 2

The best . . . Elaine Paige at the presentations last night

Theatre

'Evita'—a musical extraordinary

By *JOHN BARBER*

TWO STARS dominate "Evita," the extraordinarily successful new musical at the Prince Edward about Eva Peron, the back-street hustler who became the saint of a South American republic somewhat to the right of Caligula's Rome.

The first is Elaine Paige. She creates a woman at once brassy, steely, tinny —and human. "All I want," she sings in a sure and soaring soprano that is one of the delights of the night, "is a whole lot of excess."

The new girl gives us a high-flying beauty of unusual swagger and cynicism who instructs her entourage: "They need to adore me— so Christian Dior me!" She proceeds to scratch her way to become Argentina's instant queen.

EXPRESS AT THE BIG NIGHT

Little Elaine, you're great!

By HERBERT KRETZMER

OPERA has always been a dirty word at the box office but if EVITA doesn't give it a good name, then nothing else will.

Yes, it was worth waiting for. No, there has never been another musical quite like it. And in Elaine Paige, little in stature, and certainly no classical beauty, the show discovers a genuinely gifted new star with a voice of soaring clarity, a voice made in heaven.

On a largely-bare stage, dominated by mountainous steel girders and a giant cinema screen, Miss Paige acts, with appropriate gravity and fire, the tawdry, tragic tale of the ex-actress who became a goddess to the unthinking hordes of Argentina.

Don't cry for the new superstar

FAME AT HER FINGERTIPS Elaine Paige as Eva who stepped out of the shadows at last night's preview.

EVENING STANDARD, FEBRUARY 6, 1979

NEWS ON CAMERA

The Evita girl is a certain winner

By Sydney Edwards

THE FIRST preview of the controversial musical Evita last night confounded the critics by taking five curtain calls and leaving the invited audience baying for more.

It was a remarkable triumph for the £400,000 show's little-known star Elaine Paige, singing Eva Peron.

She undoubtedly stole the limelight from David Essex, who had been top-billed in the role of Che Guevara by producer Hal Prince.

There had been five curtain calls when the specially painted frontcloth came down and the house lights went up. But hardly a single person in the audience of 1500 moved.

I'm sure the show will run —it's a good story and even if you're not interested in history, the music really makes it.

For people who lived through the events, history has lost none of its flavour in the staging.

Colonel Ronnie Hoare 64, and up from his home in Wiltshire for the night, said : It brings back all the old memories. I think this is a tremendous show for my generation.

The show which stars David Essex and Jos Ackland has already taken £230,000 in advance bookings.

Evita stars share award

by Sydney Edwards

ELAINE PAIGE and David Essex today shared the Variety Club's top honour for their performances in the musical Evita. They were named joint show business personalities of 1978.

Lord Delfont presented the awards at a Savoy lunch.

Winners in other entertainment categories were : Peter Ustinov (best film actor for his performance in Death on the Nile); Glenda Jackson (best film actress for her performance in House Calls, Stevie and The Class of Miss MacMichael); Tom Conti (best stage actor for his performance in Whose Life is it Anyway); Felicity Kendal (best stage actress for her performance in Clouds by Michael Frayn).

Among television awards, the team in the series All Creatures Great and Small were named joint BBC TV personalities of 1978 Francesca Annis was named ITV personality for her series Lillie.

ELAINE PAIGE—Evita brings her award

Above: Reviews reprinted in the Evita *programme.*

Above: Reading the Evita *reviews the next morning. I can't believe it. Elaine Paige is on the front page!*

Below: With Joss Ackland at the Evita *album signing at Liberty's in Regent Street. To date it has sold over half a million copies.*

Left: Meeting HRH Princess Anne at the Royal Gala performance of Evita.

Below: In my dressing room at the Prince Edward Theatre with Prime Minister James Callaghan, showing him the join.

Above: With Peter Ustinov and Glenda Jackson after winning Showbusiness Personality of the Year. What a thrill!

Above: The great musical theatre actress Evelyn Laye presented me with a SWET (Society of West End Theatre) Award for Best Actress in a Musical, 1978. And a lot of sweat went into it. I dropped two dress sizes!

Below: Sharing a glass of champagne with the then Sir Laurence Olivier. Thankfully, the SWET awards are now named after him.

Left: Singing Don't Cry for Me Argentina *at Andrew Lloyd Webber's 50th birthday concert at the Royal Albert Hall, London, 1998.*

Below: With Antonio Banderas after playing Eva to his Che at Andrew's birthday concert. It was the first time he'd ever sung in public in the UK. He went on, of course, to play Che in the movie version of Evita.

*Above: Meeting Her Majesty the Queen after the Royal Variety
Performance at the Theatre Royal Drury Lane, 1981. Also in the line-
up are (left to right) Patti Boulaye, Kenny Lynch, Suzanne Danielle,
Lenny Henry and Stephanie Lawrence.*

*Above: Meeting HRH the Princess of Wales at the Birthright Charity
Concert, 1987. Left to right: Cilla Black, Dame Edna Everage (Barry
Humphries) and my* Cats *co-star Wayne Sleep.*

Above: With HRH Princess Margaret and, in the background, Russ Abbott, after the Children's Royal Variety Performance, 1991.

Above: With HRH the Prince of Wales after the Royal Variety Performance, 2000.

5

Cats

Book: Based on Old Possum's Book of Practical Cats *by T S Eliot*

Lyrics: T S Eliot
(additional lyrics by Don Black and Trevor Nunn)

Music: Andrew Lloyd Webber

New London Theatre, 1981

Abbacadabra

Book: David Wood, based on a story by Alain and Daniel Boublil

Lyrics: Don Black
(additional lyrics by Mike Batt and Björn Ulvaeus)

Music: Benny Andersson and Björn Ulvaeus (Abba)

Lyric Theatre Hammersmith, 1983

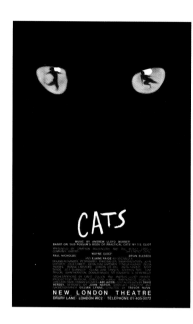

WHEN I LEFT the cast of *Evita*, for the next few months offers to play every dictator's wife known to man came flooding in, all of which I turned down. After a 20-month run, physically and mentally exhausted, I decided I needed time to rest and recover. I was financially more secure for the first time in my life, so I could afford to be more selective. But after six months' 'resting', I remembered Hal Prince warning me that I was lucky to find even one role like Evita in a career, let alone two. So I started to get a trifle jittery. Was that it? Was I a one-hit wonder?

I'm not all that superstitious, but in a strange way fate took a hand. I was driving home one night, listening to the radio. I heard a fragment of *Memory*, and the DJ said 'I'll play the whole of Andrew Lloyd Webber's theme from his new musical, *Cats*, after the midnight news'. The tune so gripped me, I dived out of the car and ran towards the house to tape the music. Fumbling for my keys, I see a mangy, thin black cat pathetically struggling toward me. A poor little stray, it begins to rub up against my ankles. At that moment, I remembered what my mother always said: 'If a black cat crosses your path, it's good luck'. So there I was, hovering at the front door, waiting for the cat to pass by. Once it had, I hurried into the house, turned on the recorder and taped

Right: With the young producer Cameron Mackintosh.

Memory. In such a hurry, I'd left the door wide open. I turned round and saw that the black cat had followed me indoors.

That night I took my Sony Walkman to bed and played the tune over and over again. I'd given the black cat some milk and I allowed her to sleep on my bed. *Memory* is such a haunting ballad, with an operatic climax in true Andrew Lloyd Webber style. It ends with an emotional expression of hope:

> 'If you touch me, you'll understand what happiness is.
> Look, a new day has begun!'

It was my kind of song! I was determined to ring Andrew the very next morning to ask, plead even, to be allowed to record it, even though I had nothing to do with the show. I fell asleep with the earphones in and the tune still wafting through my brain.

In the morning I was woken by the phone. It was the producer, Cameron Mackintosh, asking me to meet Trevor Nunn and Gillian Lynne. *Cats* was about to start previews in a few days' time and they had a problem. Judi Dench, who was to play Grizabella, had torn her Achilles tendon and was in hospital. Could I take over? At such short notice I was apprehensive, but Cameron explained apologetically that the role of Grizabella, unlike *Evita*, was a cameo.

Below: Grizabella – me in my dressing room mirror, during my weekend of rehearsals – I thought I'd better see if the costume and wig would fit!

Above and opposite: Memory –
*'I remember the time I knew what
happiness was. Let the memory
live again.'*

Below: Andrew with me at the Cats
*first night party, after a bomb scare had
disrupted the first performance.*

'Has she got a song?', I asked.
'Yes.'
'It wouldn't be called *Memory* by any chance, would it?'
'Yes. It's the only song she has.'

But what a song! I needed no more persuasion.

I joined a great ensemble cast; big, blustering Brian Blessed, Shakespearean actor and mountaineer, played Deuteronomy; tiny Wayne Sleep, the smallest dancer ever to get into the Royal Ballet School, a non-stop talker with phenomenal energy, played Mister Mistoffelees; Rum Tum Tugger was played by my old friend, Paul Nicholas – the only leading man to work with me four times and survive! Younger cats were played by Bonnie Langford, Finola Hughes, and Sarah Brightman no less.

Singing *Memory* turned out to be a feat of memory. The lyrics were changing from night to night. The director Trevor Nunn, Tim Rice and Don Black all had a hand in it until Trevor's original lyric, inspired by lines from T S Eliot's *Rhapsody on a Windy Night*, prevailed.

Cats was another ground-breaking British musical. No one had seen anything quite like it. A cast of actors, singers and dancers created believable animal characters, long before *The Lion King*. We *became* cats. Gillian Lynne made us study cat behaviour, mimic their movements to help us bring to life the alien feline world from a cat's point of view. A legendary dancer herself, Gillian was associate director and choreographed the show. *Cats* won her an Olivier Award for Outstanding Achieve-

Above left: Grizabella – the kitten.

Above right: Memory – *'I was beautiful then.'*

ment of the Year in Musicals, and the Broadway production won seven Tony awards.

By the time *Cats* opened on Broadway I'd already left the London cast. It was a lonely nine months playing the outcast, Grizabella. Always on stage alone, every time I came on the company left, and when they returned I limped away into the wings. I went to my dressing room to wait for my next entrance. It was like being in solitary confinement. I knew that nine months would be enough, and so it proved; though if the chance to play Grizabella on Broadway had been offered to me, I would have gone. I loved the old cat and the song.

Grizabella, 'the glamour cat', has such a poignant moment near the end of the show, the climactic number, known in the profession as the 'the eleven o'clock number'. She stands alone amid the magnified rubbish dump, brilliantly designed by John Napier. She sees a kitten and tries to dance along with her. Now old and weary, she reflects on the life of glamour that she had once known and sings *Memory*.

Memory brought the house down. Fate had handed it to me on a saucer! I was the first Grizabella. Since then, however, I'm told, that more than 150 artists have recorded versions of *Memory*. But I'm possessive and I still see it as my signature.

Cats ran for 21 years in the West End. Until recently, it was the longest running show in history, an accolade now passed on to *Les Misérables*, by me when I handed my cat skin (the baton!) to a *Les Mis* waif. The 'ceremony' took place after a performance at the Queens Theatre, Shaftesbury Avenue, on 7 October 2006.

PS: The 'lucky' black cat stayed with me for the rest of her life. At first, I called her Prince, after Hal, but after the success of *Cats* I simply had to rename her Grizabella.

Me with my best boy 'Tugger' — named after Rum Tum Tugger of course! I'd only have to mention the word 'cats' and he'd be off. I think he was so insulted to be named after a cat.

Abbacadabra

Lightning strikes twice: another call from Cameron Mackintosh. This time it's a children's Christmas play with music, called *Abbacadabra*. I immediately think of pantomime. No thanks. I'd done panto early in my career, including *Babes in the Wood* at the London Palladium – a Christmas season that lasted till Easter! Twice daily! The best thing about *Babes in the Wood* for me was the tremendous cast, which included Arthur Askey, Roy Castle, Roy Kinnear, and 'I remember Yoohoo!' Frank Ifield.

However, there was an upside to *Abbacadabra*. It was a very good script by David Wood, renowned for his children's plays and stories. The music was a compilation of Abba hits by Benny Andersson and Björn Ulvaeus; a forerunner of the compilation shows that young people flock to today. Once again, I'm in an exciting, innovative new musical.

Right: With 'Big-Hearted' Arthur Askey. I did the panto Babes in the Wood *with him.*

Below: As Carabosse in Abbacadabra.

The story begins in a school classroom. It's the dawn of the computer age, and I play the dual role of the prim schoolteacher, Miss Williams, and her alter-ego, the punk witch, Carabosse. Miss Williams dismisses the class and leaves, but the children stay behind and log on to the computer. Suddenly they are transported into cyberspace. A modern take on *Through the Looking Glass*, the *Wizard of Oz*, or *The Lion, the Witch and the Wardrobe* in which children are also transported to another world. I'd always wanted to fly on stage. As Carabosse, I flew in astride a Harley Davidson motorbike, dressed from head to toe in leather, a fantastic costume designed by Sue Blane. My last song was another strong ballad, *Like an Image Passing By*, and at the end I disappeared in a puff of smoke.

Fantastic Abba songs, with new lyrics by Don Black, outrageous wigs, and funky costumes. I loved it. *Abbacadabra* ran for eight weeks. By that time it was a year since Abba had given their last performance together. But I was to work with Benny and Björn again on their rock opera masterpiece, *Chess*.

Abbacadabra has never seen another production, but it paved the way for another Abba compilation show, *Mamma Mia*.

The Lyric Theatre
Hammersmith
by arrangement with
**Cameron
Mackintosh**
presents

ABBACADABRA

8 December 1983 –
21 January 1984

FINANCIALLY ASSISTED
Hammersmith
& Fulham   GLC funded

Lyric Theatre Hammersmith
King Street, London W6

In my Carabosse incarnation, with B A Robertson as 'Beast'.

Above: In the dock as Kate Webster in 'Not for the Nervous', part of the series Lady Killers *for Granada TV (1980).*

Below: In the cells with Peter Sallis and Michael Kitchen.

Above and below: With Lewis Collins in the TV musical A Night on the Town *(1983). In this piece I played four different roles in four different cities: above, as a hat-check girl in New York; and below, playing a Southern Belle in a brothel, with Eartha Kitt as the madame.*

6

Chess

Book and Lyrics: Tim Rice

Music: Benny Andersson and Björn Ulvaeus (Abba)

Prince Edward Theatre, London, 1986

Anything Goes

Book: Timothy Crouse and John Weidman,
based on an original story by
P G Wodehouse & Guy Bolton,
and Howard Lindsay & Russel Crouse

Music and Lyrics: Cole Porter

Prince Edward Theatre, London, 1989

Chess

CHESS

PRINCE EDWARD THEATRE

A LOVE TRIANGLE during the world chess championship in Merano, Northern Italy. I played Florence Vassey, assistant ('the second') to a temperamental American chess champion, played by Murray Head, who is defending his title against a young Russian challenger, played by Tommy Körberg. The stage is set for a battle of minds in an atmosphere of mutual loathing. Walkouts, insults and a complete breakdown of relations fuel a tense dramatic 'cold war' between the players. They abandon the match. As Florence, the peacemaker, tries to bring the two players back togther, she finds herself attracted to the young Russian contender. It was a difficult role, rather too close to home. At the time I was in love with the extremely married Tim Rice.

Tim had wanted to write a show for me, so the historical rock musical, *Blondel*, was definitely written with me mind. Unfortunately, he'd overlooked the fact that the central character, Blondel, was a man, the troubadour in King Richard the Lionheart's court. I didn't connect with Stephen Oliver's music either. None of my objections went down well with Tim. The role of

Fiona, a medieval 'political activist', centuries ahead of her time, just didn't interest me. To me, *Blondel* was like a musical history lesson, an educational musical, excellent for schools, but not for me. After nearly a year at the Old Vic it transferred to the Aldwych Theatre for a further eight months.

Chess was also written with me in mind, and was a project in which I was involved from its inception. Like *Jesus Christ Superstar* and *Evita*, it began as a concept album. I would accompany Tim on weekend visits to Stockholm to work in Abba's famous Polar Recording Studios. With Benny, Björn, Tim and Tommy, we tried out different tunes, keys and lyrics; swapped around duets and solos. It was a workshop, a new experience for me to be part of the creative process. The passionate soaring melodies rolled like waves from Benny's fingers. In fact one of my favourite demos was called *When the Waves Roll Out to Sea*: amazingly this emotional ballad never made it into the original production.

Above: Tim and me at Air Studios, Oxford Circus, London.

Left: The poster for Tim's musical Blondel.

Opposite: With Benny Andersson, Tim Rice and Björn Ulvaeus.

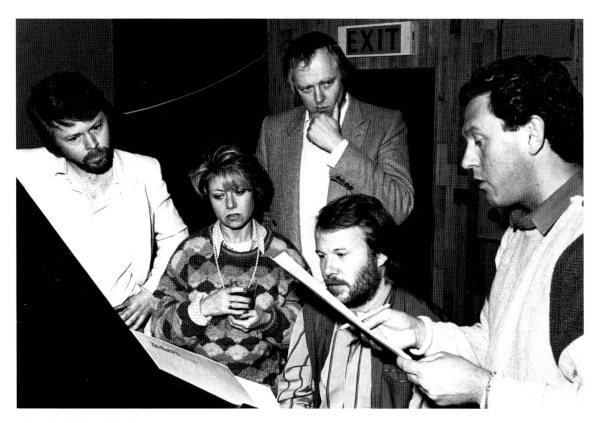

Above: With Björn, Tim, Benny and Tommy Körberg running through the song You and I *at Polar Studios, Stockholm, from whence came all the Abba hits we know and love.*

Below and opposite: With Tommy recording at the Polar Studios.

The album was released in 1984, coinciding with a European concert tour, singing with the London Symphony Orchestra, a fifty-strong choir, and a rock band joined by Benny and Björn themselves. Quite an experience.

Right: On of the cars which travelled us around Europe on the album launch tour. Saab-Scania were the sponsors.

Below: With my pal Barbara Dickson – we'd just got to Number 1 in the charts with our single I Know Him so Well *and we're being presented with a disc each in recognition of sales over 500,000.*

The *Chess* album got into the UK top forty chart, and the single of *I Know Him so Well*, a duet for Barbara Dickson and me, climbed to Number 1 in the British charts for four weeks. Every Friday night, we were on the phone eagerly studying form. We've been on the phone ever since.

Above: A rare picture of us all together taken for the Sunday Times. *Moody or what?!*

Almost two years after the release of the concept album, Murray Head, Tommy Körberg and I recreate the roles on the stage in the West End at the Prince Edward Theatre. There are new songs and additional plot, and the previously unnamed American and Russian characters are now Frederick Trumper and Anatoly Sergievsky.

This is the eighties: there's a lot of money around and everything is big, brash and bold. Shows are extravagant and *Chess* is one of the most extravagant to date. Everything is high-tech sets and hydraulics. The show opens with a human chess game played out on an illuminated chessboard that lifts and tilts; the proscenium is flanked by banks of television monitors broadcasting news bulletins and chess commentaries.

Below: As Florence Vassey singing Nobody's Side *onstage in Chess, Prince Edward Theatre, 1986.*

To sing that score every night was a joy and many funny moments occurred throughout the run. The set was a hydraulic mountain that tilted forward towards the audience at a 1:4 incline. At one performance Murray Head was meant to have climbed up onto the mountain from a ladder backstage. He missed his footing. One moment his head appeared and then he was gone. It was a comic sight. Subsequently we had to wear thick rubber soles on our shoes to stop us sliding down the perspex mountain. One night Tommy Körberg and I were gazing into each other's eyes during a love scene (*see below*), when whilst singing he accidentally spat at me in both eyes. It was such a shock my eyes closed shut and I got a fit of the giggles, so what should have been a tender heartfelt love scene, disintegrated into helpless laughter.

Below: On stage with Tommy in Chess. *Art mirroring life!*

Above: With Tim and Benny opposite the Prince Edward Theatre, the day it was announced a mystery computer fault had scuppered the £4 million opening of Chess.

Anything Goes

Washington 1988: I was there to sing in concert at the White House for President and Nancy Reagan. In New York, a revival of Cole Porter's 1930s musical *Anything Goes*, starring Patti Lupone is a big hit at the Lincoln Center's Vivian Beaumont Theatre. So I had to see it. Patti had shot to stardom in the Broadway production of *Evita*.

Anything Goes was a knockout. It has some of the best music and lyrics that anyone would ever want to sing. In addition to the title song there is a string of classic numbers, *I Get a Kick out of You, Easy to Love, It's de-Lovely, You're the Top, All Through the Night, Friendship,* and *Blow, Gabriel, Blow!* I came out of the Lincoln Centre Theatre smiling from ear to ear. A jewel of a traditional American musical comedy; witty, energetic and slick. The central part of Reno Sweeney is a gift of a comic role, something I'd yet to tackle in a 'serious' way. I'd touched on it

Left: With theatre proprietor and impresario Bernard Delfont, proving 'Anything Goes'.

Above: A fan gave me this doll. It was meant to be a lookalike…it's up to you!

Below: On stage during the comic tango with Martin Turner.

with Rita in *Billy* and Madcap Maisie in *The Boyfriend*, but this was a starring role. What a change from the tragic women I'd played so far! Now I had the chance to surprise people as a comedienne playing a brassy, warm-hearted flirt. I knew instantly that I wanted to do it in the West End. But how? Was there a plan to bring the production to London? If so, would I get the role? Well, you know what they say: 'If you want something done…' So I became a producer!

In New York I had been hob-nobbing with the great and the good – partying in Andrew Lloyd Webber's penthouse in the Trump Tower, Fifth Avenue, along with Tim Rice, Sarah Brightman, and Bob Geldof. I was getting lofty ideas! That evening my personal assistant Kate Weston and I talked of little else but the show. It became obvious that, to make certain I played the role, there was no other way but to produce it myself.

Back in London, I got to work and before long I was co–producing with Tim Rice and Robert Fox. We secured the rights to the American production. A date was set. Jerry Zaks, the director of the New York production agreed to mount the production in the West End. The entire American team came to London, excluding the cast, except for Howard McGillin who played Billy Crocker. Jerry knew what he wanted. He knew what worked. We held auditions at the Royalty Theatre, Kingsway. We were up and running. The show opened at the Prince Edward

Left: Reno making up to Billy (Howard McGillin). It wasn't hard – he was so cute.

Theatre on 4th July 1989, American Independence Day. But independence brings responsibility, and this was to be one of the most stressful, yet exciting periods in my career.

An instant conflict of interest set in between myself as a performer and wearing my other hat as practical, cost-conscious producer. I was now seeing things, not just from an artistic point of view, but also through the balance sheet. Casting was another eye-opener. I could consider the whole production process from a completely new perspective, and realised something about casting that I had never quite come to terms with as a performer. Sitting in on auditions, I could see that it's easier to direct an actor whose natural characteristics chime with those of the character in the play. As a director, you need an instinct to spot the right person for the role.

A good example is the casting of John Barrowman to take over from Howard McGillin as Billy Crocker.

Below: With Bernard Cribbins and a young John Barrowman, who had just joined the Anything Goes *company as Billy. Mayhem ensued nightly.*

John *was* Billy Crocker. He had the self-confidence, charm and swagger – braggadocio! We assembled a great cast. Veteran actor Bernard Cribbins played the gangster, Moonface Martin; the rest of the cast included Kathryn Evans, Ursula Smith, Ashleigh Sendin, Martin Turner and Harry Towb.

The story is set aboard the SS American on a voyage from New York to England. A ship full of larger-than-life characters, romantically entangled but 'shipwrecked' by mistaken identities. At the centre of the mayhem is tough cookie, Reno Sweeney, an unlikely evangelist-turned-nightclub hostess. The role not only gave me some of the best songs any singer could wish for, but also the chance to dance up a storm – a five-minute-long tap number to the title song *Anything Goes* – a real test of stamina, brilliantly choreographed by Michael Smuin. His witty tango was another gift! I danced it with the English toff, played by Martin Turner, and it brought the house down nightly.

Below: Bill Hewison's cartoon of Anything Goes *for* Punch.

ANYTHING GOES —
BERNARD CRIBBINS as Moonface Martin
MARTIN TURNER as Lord Evelyn Oakleigh
ELAINE PAIGE as Reno Sweeney
HOWARD McGILLIN as Billy Crocker
— Prince Edward Theatre
Punch issue : 14 July 1989

Above: With Bernard Cribbins, Howard McGillin and Her Majesty Queen Elizabeth the Queen Mother, 1989. Reviews were good, so was word of mouth and a month into the run we were honoured with a royal visit. The Queen Mother, a great Cole Porter fan, had asked to see Anything Goes *for her 89th birthday. At the end of the performance, I'm summoned to the royal box to be presented. I'd sung, danced and tapped my way through the entire evening, but still I race upstairs puffing and panting. The Lady-in-Waiting introduces us with the awesome words 'Her Majesty Queen Elizabeth The Queen Mother'. I take her hand, sink into a formal deep curtsy and get cramp! I'm stuck! I look up into Her Majesty's eyes, my face contoted with horror, gasping. 'Your Majesty…' Wobbling helplessly as I cling to the great lady's hand I nearly nearly bring her down with me. There's a surreal moment of low eye contact between us. Is this really happening? And then, to my amazement, with a sudden burst of superhuman strength, she hoists me up. Stunned silence. The Lady-in-Waiting, the theatre manager, the bodyguard, even the Queen Mother look at me with a mixture of pity and disbelief. Finally the Queen Mother breaks the silence and says, 'I thought that only happened at my age'.*

Above: Tony Walton's design for Reno Sweeney's red dress in Anything Goes.

Opposite: The red dress in action during the song Blow, Gabriel, Blow. *'A cleavage shaped like the Grand Canyon', according to Maureen Paton!*

Above: With Diana Rigg on the set of the BBC TV drama
Unexplained Laughter *(1988). We couldn't film this scene for*
laughing until the directors told us we'd have to pay the crews overtime!
That did it!

Below: The night shoot starts to wear thin – taking a break in my
trailer (in the days when it wasn't illegal to smoke indoors…).

Above: As the wife of the depressive alcoholic Harry Clark played by Griff Rhys Jones in the BBC film A View of Harry Clark *(1989).*

Below: In A Murder is Announced (*Granada/WGBH, 2005). Much fun was had with Zoë Wanamaker and Geraldine McEwan as Miss Marple. What a glamorous trio!*

7

Piaf

Written by: Pam Gems

The Peter Hall Company

Piccadilly Theatre, 1993

FRENCH POPULAR songs are mostly written for the French. Certain great French singers transcend the language barrier. Maurice Chevalier, Jacques Brel, Johnny Hallyday, Charles Aznavour are among the best known French male singers outside France. Among the chanteuses, perhaps only Edith Piaf has achieved international fame with hits like *Mon legionnaire*, *L'accordéoniste*, *La vie en rose*, *Non, je ne regrette rien*, and *Milord*, which made the British charts in 1960.

Many of Piaf's songs are typically French in telling tragic stories. They echo the feelings and language of ordinary people, describing scenes of real life misery and deprivation. But for Piaf there was also laughter and joy when she lived among her friends, the artists and musicians of Montmartre and La Pigalle.

The accordion is a familiar sound in the streets of Paris. The songs, and the sound of the accordion feature in many of the arrangements: one of her best known songs being *L'accordéoniste*, by Michel Emer, which tells a sad story about street life. Emer was a young bespectacled Jewish boy. He brought the song to the Bobino theatre on the eve of the premiere of her new season and refused to leave until she had listened to it. It was the first of her records to sell over a million copies. He was to write over 30 more songs for her.

Opposite: As Piaf.

Among her favourite composers and lyricists were Marguerite Monnot, Georges Moustaki, Michel Vaucair, Charles Aznavour and Charles Dumont, whose *Non, je ne regrette rien* put her career back on the map after a period in decline. Her own life was as tragic as her songs: a cycle of broken relationships, drugs and disappointments. Piaf co-wrote with Marguerite Monnot the soul searing *L'hymne à l'amour* after her lover, the boxer Marcel Cerdan, died in a plane crash en route to see her in New York. But singing was her salvation: 'For me singing is a way of escaping. It's another world. I am no longer on earth'.

A tiny, fragile figure on stage, always dressed in a simple black dress, she was the embodiment of her own repertoire. Indeed, she said so herself: 'If people want to know about me, they need only listen to my songs.' She had risen from poverty, a street urchin who fought hard for everything she achieved. Not for her the sequins and glamour of showbiz. It was all in the voice and the way she interpreted her songs with such passion. The voice itself was extraordinarily powerful, a haunting fusion of sound and emotion.

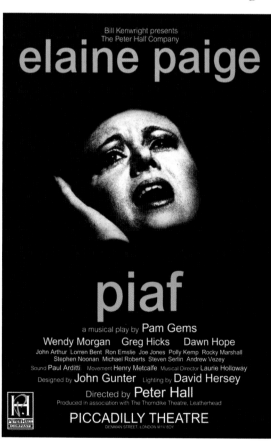

Bill Kenwright presents
The Peter Hall Company

elaine paige

piaf

a musical play by **Pam Gems**

Wendy Morgan   Greg Hicks   Dawn Hope

John Arthur Lorren Bent Ron Emslie Joe Jones Polly Kemp Rocky Marshall
Stephen Noonan Michael Roberts Steven Serlin Andrew Vezey

Sound **Paul Arditti**   Movement **Henry Metcalfe**   Musical Director **Laurie Holloway**

Designed by **John Gunter**   Lighting by **David Hersey**

Directed by **Peter Hall**

Produced in association with The Thorndike Theatre, Leatherhead

PICCADILLY THEATRE

DENMAN STREET, LONDON W1V 8DY

But there is a lot more to Piaf than the songs. She was born Edith Giovanna Gassion. Her mother was a prostitute and sometime café singer. Her father was a street acrobat. The young Piaf would take round the hat to collect a few coins to earn a meagre living. One day when her father was too ill to perform, Piaf launched into song instead. They collected more money than ever before, and so by chance Piaf's singing career began on the streets of Paris. Imagine today any singer performing in the London underground becoming a legend and you have some idea of the leap Piaf made from street singer to international recording artist. Imagine, too, how passionate she was about everything in her life, above all the music and the men. This passion lives on in Pam Gems' extraordinary play, *Piaf.* The play is not just a biopic with little more than the storyline and the music. There is a real character for an actress to explore.

Pam wrote the play for Magdalena Busnia, an actress who, unable to find work in London, was singing Piaf's songs outside the underground at Oxford Circus. 'At the time, says Pam Gems, 'I was working with Ed Berman at the Almost Free Theatre and Ed suggested I wrote a play about Piaf for Magdalena. Although I wasn't enthusiastic about the idea, Magdalena was. She turned up with her son at my house in Kensington, saying she had nowhere to go. So I took her in and from then on she bullied me to write *Piaf.* But my agent's opinion was damning. He didn't believe it would work with a cockney Edith Piaf. So I put the script away and forgot about it.'

Then Pam saw me in *Billy* at Drury Lane in 1974. In Pam's words: 'I've found Piaf! There she was, tiny, looking very young, and with a sodding great voice!'

Four years later a copy of the script had found its way to the RSC. The role was first played by Jane Lapotaire in the RSC production in 1978. She

NO REGRETS: The real Piaf

Paige soars as the Little Sparrow Piaf

PIAF — Piccadilly Theatre, London

WHO could resist the tiny, indomitable Elaine Paige as the tiny, indomitable Edith Piaf, singing that defiant Norman Lamont song, Je Ne Regrette Rien? Not me, for one — nor the jam-packed West End theatre that gave her a standing ovation for her gutsiness in Sir Peter Hall's stylish revival of Pam Gems's musical play.

Jane Lapotaire won a Tony Award during the Broadway transfer when she played the title role in the original RSC production more than a decade ago.

But hold on to your seatbelts: Paige IS Piaf in an astonishing incarnation of the foul-mouthed, fascinating Little Sparrow.

Piaf, a street singer plucked from the gutter, was France's most famous chanteuse, drug addict, toy-boy collector and superstar. She had more to regret than most, but Piaf characteristically never gave a damn.

She certainly never stopped being a guttersnipe, and some Paige fans may have a fit of the vapours at the number of four-letter words their heroine manages to fit in between songs.

Yet she is tremendous in the role — vibrant, funny, earthy, tender and raucous by turns, a hellcat with a sense of humour.

Vitality

We all know about the stupendous voice — and Paige's powerful renditions of the majestic Mon Dieu and Je Ne Regrette Rien duly raise the rafters — but it's easy to overlook what a strong dramatic actress Paige is.

There is nothing remotely ingratiating about her take-it-or-leave-it, deglamorised performance, as direct and tough and uncompromising as Piaf herself. Yet her unstoppable vitality endears her to us and makes us care.

This is not a great play. Gems presents Piaf's short life in a rapid succession of sketchy scenes that depict her as endlessly hungry for love but never delve deeply into her rebellious psychology.

Her harem of men are a pretty interchangeable lot. Only Wendy Morgan makes a real impact as Piaf's tarty, hard-headed friend Toine.

Essentially it's a star vehicle for an overwhelming personality — and Paige has that in abundance.

My only regret is that we never actually hear her sing that peerless Piaf number La Vie En Rose, though the on-stage band strikes up the first bars several times. Criminal to miss such an opportunity for an encore.

MAUREEN PATON

ASTONISHING: Elaine as the legendary Edith Picture: STEVE WOOD

won a Tony Award for her Broadway performance in 1981. Sadly, I never saw her because I was in *Evita*.

That didn't stop me wanting to play it when the opportunity arose fifteen years later. I read the play at the suggestion of my agent, James Sharkey, and liked it so much I bought a three-year option on it. Just as I knew I could play Eva Peron, I knew instantly how much the role of Piaf would suit me. It's not just that I'm the same height as Eva Peron and Edith Piaf, or that my initials are the same as both women! But like Piaf my voice is strongest in the middle register. With my 'producer's' experience on *Anything Goes* under my belt I knew a bit more about getting things on. I approached Peter Hall, whose company (The Peter Hall Company) was in partnership with producer Bill Kenwright. Peter agreed to direct. We opened at the Thorndike Theatre, Leatherhead and toured for six weeks prior to the West End opening at the Piccadilly Theatre. The cast included Greg Hicks, Wendy Morgan and Dawn Hope. Adrian Mitchell wrote new English lyrics.

I needed to learn more about her life and the kind of world she lived in. So I went to Paris, armed with a map and a camera to explore the streets where Piaf had lived. It was already well known that as a young girl she lived rough, but I needed more to build a fully rounded character. So, first, I made an appointment to visit the 'Piaf' private museum, run by Bernard Marchois, located in a two-room apartment in the Belleville district. Marchois

Above: Visiting Belleville, birthplace of Edith Piaf.

Left: At the Piaf Museum.

knew Piaf during the last few years of her life and since then has kept this shrine to her memory. It was a revelation. The walls are covered in gold and platinum albums, paintings from her art collection, private correspondence, some of her furniture, photographs and other memorabilia; but of special importance to me, soon to play the part of Piaf, I felt in touch with her spirit from the moment I set eyes on her clothes, shoes, gloves, handbags and, of course, the famous little black dress which she always wore on stage. If I had put them on myself there and then, they would have fitted me. I was becoming *her!* Perhaps it's the sleuth in me that compels me to do so much research, but it was well worth it.

Next stop; to meet Charles Dumont, the composer of *Non, je ne regrette rien.* Like Michael Emer before him, Dumont had to force his way into Piaf's repertoire by waiting outside her door to play his song for her. And what a song! It would be the song to revitalise her career. It became her signature tune. Dumont asked me to sing it in his apartment. It was only when he began to play the introduction that I realised what I had let myself in for. What nerve! This was the composer himself and here was I daring to follow in Piaf's footsteps, singing in French! I gripped the edge of the piano, and hit that first 'Non!' with all the nasal power I could muster. The defiant spirit of the song, 'no regrets!', builds in intensity to the very end, and so did I, still gripping the piano. I think I left indelible fingerprints there. By then, Dumont was beaming and shouting 'Ah, oui! Ah, oui!' Audition over. I was home and dry.

Opposite: Piaf's black dress.

Below: With Charles Dumont, the composer of Non, je ne regrette rien.

Back in London I interviewed Charles Aznavour over breakfast at the Savoy. At first he seemed sceptical, but breakfast became lunch as he excitedly relived his first-hand recollections of Piaf. There were so many wonderful tales, but a few stick in my mind. Before he became a singer himself, Aznavour worked with Piaf and would drive her to venues. She also made him drive fast, the faster and more dangerous the better, and she awarded him stars for 'success'. They had their rituals, too. They sang all the way, the same three songs, one of which was *My Yiddishe Momme*. Humour was as much part of her life as sadness. 'Everything with her was a contradiction,' he said. 'She lived her life between tears and laughter.' On the bright side, Piaf always made a joke as she left a room and would walk out laughing. She wanted to part on a happy note. But of her early life on the streets, Aznavour recalls that she washed herself in the fountain in the Place de la Concorde and dried herself with newspaper, so she ended up grubbier than she was in the first place. This hardship aside, it must be said that Piaf loved the freedom of street life and, even after she became a star, she often returned to the bars and cafés of La Pigalle, the district where she perfected her art. Here she could hang out with her 'real' friends. Indeed, all her life, she snubbed those she described as 'l'honorable Société'.

Above: With Charles Aznavour at the Savoy Hotel, London. The French singing star and one-time 'dangerous driver' for Edith Piaf.

Below: Still from LWT's South Bank Show, *1995.*

Société, it seems, wasn't all bad. She met Jean Cocteau, who became a close friend. In turn, Cocteau baptised her 'the poet of the streets' and she became the darling of the intellectuals. Edith Piaf asked Cocteau to write something for her and the outcome was *Le bel indifferent* (known in English as *Duet for One Voice.*) Based on what she had told him of her life with the actor-singer, Paul Meurisse. It was performed in February, 1940, as an afterpiece to the author's *Les monstres sacrés* at the Théâtre des Bouffes-Parisiens, with Paul Meurisse playing the man for the first few weeks. Although Piaf triumphed in the part, she initially found it very difficult and wished to give it up. She was persuaded not to by Yvonne de Bray, who was playing the leading part in *Les Monstres Sacrés* and who coached her personally. The

production ran for three months until world events forced it to close, but, although it was well-received, the audience's response was muted. They left the theatre in silence, feeling, as Cocteau put it, 'as though they had been looking through a keyhole'.

Piaf was a perfectionist and thoughtful, and would spend hours working out one gesture to express the lyric and mood of a song. Below is an edited extract from Pam Gems' play. It allows Piaf to speak directly to us:

> 'Where's the follow spot? I'm not *that* small!
>
> Just do what you're paid for.
>
> It's the same every time, just before you go on.
>
> Never mind what they've said to you in the dressing room – your mates.
>
> That walk to the mike, it's from here to Rome.
>
> And if you screw up, well, you can't say 'ang on, loves. Mind if I have another go?
>
> Well, I have been known to.
>
> No, even worse, if it's gone off well. You don't want it to end.
>
> Show over, you're on your own again.
>
> Funny, you don't notice the pain on stage. You're up. Fired.
>
> Did a whole show once, three cracked ribs, broken ankle, neck in a brace, wore a higher collar, same black dress, higher collar.
>
> It's when you come off, that's when you pay for it.
>
> Not at me best then, I can tell yer.
>
> It's like you 'aven't left yourself enough to get by on.
>
> When I go on to do a song, they get the lot. They see what they're getting, every-thing I got.
>
> No, when I'm out there, it's *gotta* happen.'

Piaf is a hugely taxing role. Not only did I have to grapple with her despair from the age of fifteen through drugs, alcohol, the pain and angst of lost love, and the physical pain of a broken jaw, arthritis, leading to her premature death at 48 in 1963. I had to die every night. Her lifestyle killed her. Playing her life nearly killed me. This was a full-length drama with more than a dozen songs to perform in their entirety. I played six performances a week for eight months.

Above: With Spennie and Katie in my dressing room at the Novello Theatre during the run of The Drowsy Chaperone, *2007.*

Kate Weston (right) has been my personal assistant, working tirelessly with me, taking care of my diary, my office, in fact my life, for over twenty-two years. Over that time she has become my closest friend. She knows as much about my life as I do, probably more! I owe her so much. I call her 'Katherine the Great'.

Spencer Kitchen (left) has dressed me since Piaf. *She is a small strong woman with nimble fingers. Adept at the quickest of changes (our quickest was 16 seconds in the dark, during* Sunset Boulevard, *out of the leopard skin dress into a red and black trouser suit, on a small offstage tower stage right: it needed Andrew Ross and Sue Strother my wig mistress to achieve a full wig, costume and shoe change, but we always made it!), we share the same daft sense of humour and together have laughed (and cried) our way through many a show . I owe her credit for much more than just getting me on stage at the right time in the right costume.*

My long time MD and friend Laurie Holloway played the piano à la mode as he was trucked on and off stage all evening in Piaf. *You had to be there! Here we are, sharing fish and chips on tour in 1993.*

Opposite: In summer 1994, coming back from Kate Weston's wedding, on the bonnet of a Bentley. I loved having long hair.

8

Sunset Boulevard

Book and Lyrics: Don Black and Christopher Hampton,
based on the screenplay by Billy Wilder and Charles Brackett and D M Marshman Jr

Music: Andrew Lloyd Webber

Adelphi Theare, London, 1994

Sunset Boulevard

A HOLLYWOOD movie makes it to the stage, and I finally make it to Broadway – ten musicals down the line!

Sunset Boulevard is the ultimate Hollywood comeback story. Everyone remembers Gloria Swanson as Norma Desmond in the classic Billy Wilder movie, playing an ageing silent movie star, desperately trying to make her Hollywood comeback in 'talkies'. The silent movie era was over and, like the fictitious Norma Desmond, many stars had fallen into obscurity. History records that finding the lead for the movie was not easy. Several stars turned down the role, including Mary Pickford and Mae West. Playing an ageing has-been was not for them.

Opposite: With One Look.

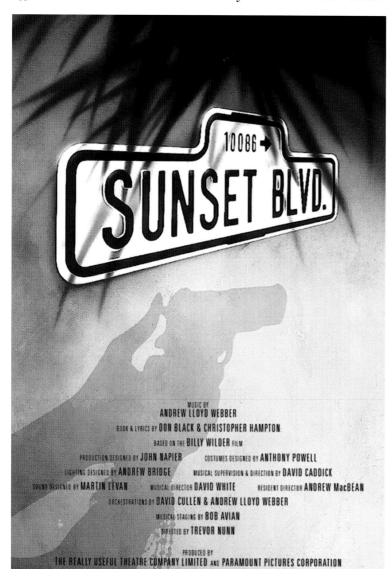

MUSIC BY
ANDREW LLOYD WEBBER
BOOK & LYRICS BY **DON BLACK & CHRISTOPHER HAMPTON.**
BASED ON THE **BILLY WILDER** FILM
PRODUCTION DESIGNED BY **JOHN NAPIER**   COSTUMES DESIGNED BY **ANTHONY POWELL**
LIGHTING DESIGNED BY **ANDREW BRIDGE**   MUSICAL SUPERVISION & DIRECTION BY **DAVID CADDICK**
SOUND DESIGNED BY **MARTIN LEVAN**   MUSICAL DIRECTOR **DAVID WHITE**   RESIDENT DIRECTOR **ANDREW MacBEAN**
ORCHESTRATIONS BY **DAVID CULLEN & ANDREW LLOYD WEBBER**
MUSICAL STAGING BY **BOB AVIAN**
DIRECTED BY **TREVOR NUNN**
PRODUCED BY
THE REALLY USEFUL THEATRE COMPANY LIMITED AND **PARAMOUNT PICTURES CORPORATION**

ADELPHI THEATRE
STRAND, LONDON WC2

My first encounter with Andrew Lloyd Webber's musical began with a call from him one Thursday evening. He was excited: 'I've written another *Memory*. I want to play it to you. Can you come over?' I dropped everything, and within an hour I was in his house in Belgrave Square. The song was called *One Small Glance* (later to become *With One Look.*). Andrew was about to be married to Madeleine Gurney and he wanted me to sing it at his wedding breakfast the following Saturday.

I needed just one hearing of *One Small Glance!* So little time to prepare! And I'm always so nervous when I don't have enough rehearsal time. But another *Memory*? How could I refuse?

The wedding breakfast was at Sydmonton Court, Berkshire, and everyone who was anyone was there. I'm joining in the fun and having a marvellous time, but then disaster strikes. Amy Powers, the lyricist, also a lawyer and writing lyrics for CBS, appears at my table and presents a new set of lyrics! I go into panic. I make a dash for my room to peruse the new lyrics, passing Andrew's famous collection of

Above: The young Norma Desmond.

Right: Norma: New Ways to Dream

pre-Raphaelite paintings. 'Oh God! Couldn't I just make a run for it?' I mutter feebly. 'Courage!' But courage to sight-read new lyrics on the spot doesn't come easily to a singer. Every song tells a story, and it takes time to find the meaning in the words and how they sit on the melody, where to breathe, where to place emphasis, how it feels in your throat. These are just a few of the considerations required to interpret the song fulsomely and to draw in your audience. Consequently, with new words, new sounds and phrasing to get to grips with, I was lost.

In *Sunset Boulevard* Andrew has created a role that no sane, singing actress would turn down, but by the time it came to cast the role of Norma Desmond, I was strutting my stuff as Edith Piaf. I was not in the running to play Norma Desmond anyway.

Left: With John Barrowman in the London production of Sunset Boulevard.

Below: Mum and Dad, my greatest supporters – always there at every opening.

The part went to Patti Lupone, followed by Betty Buckley. When, eventually, I was asked to take over from Betty Buckley I was exhausted after an eight-month run in *Piaf*, as well as in the midst of recording an album of Piaf material for Warner Brothers, so the timing wasn't right. And what about the spectacular set of *Sunset Boulevard*, a Hollywood mansion built around a magnificent staircase? Norma Desmond spends a lot of time grandly sweeping up and down those stairs, wearing heavily beaded gowns. On top of all this, I have to admit, there was a little matter of pride, having not been offered the role in the first place. Except for revivals like *Anything Goes* and *Piaf*, I now saw myself as a 'creator' of leading roles in original musicals. How wrong I was!

Having turned down the chance to play Norma Desmond, I didn't expect to be asked again, but a few months later the phone rings. It's another call from Andrew. Betty was in hospital recovering from an emergency appendectomy and would be off for six weeks over the Christmas period. They felt her fans would not be content with an understudy for that long. Casting my doubts aside, what did I have to lose?

Above left: Making up as Norma Desmond.

Above right: EP as Norma, though some thought I looked like Gloria Swanson.

Opposite: The marquee at the Minskoff Theatre, New York, 1996.

Right: The first make-up test – Norma begins to emerge.

SUNSET 10086

STARRING
ELAINE PAIGE

BOX OFFICE OPENS DAILY AT 10AM
SUNDAY AT NOON

←

TICKETMASTER "SUNSET" HOTLINE
(212) 307-4007

Broadway

TIMES
SQUARE
SUNDAY
SEPT. 8
12:30PM

RENT

24 hr.
Parking

I was being helpful to Andrew, and it was only for six weeks. Not least, it's an iconic part in modern musical theatre. Better late than never, I'm back where I belong, and how good it feels!

When Betty Buckley left the London production to take over the role on Broadway, Andrew asked me back to the Adelphi. By now, like Norma Desmond, I was 'good and ready'. Thank goodness I was.

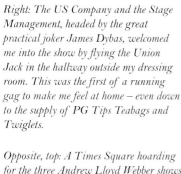

Right: The US Company and the Stage Management, headed by the great practical joker James Dybas, welcomed me into the show by flying the Union Jack in the hallway outside my dressing room. This was the first of a running gag to make me feel at home – even down to the supply of PG Tips Teabags and Twiglets.

Opposite, top: A Times Square hoarding for the three Andrew Lloyd Webber shows playing on Broadway simultaneously in 1996. What a welcome!

Six months later I, too, found myself on Broadway, as Andrew had promised. A great moment in my career as I descended the famous staircase onto the stage of the Minskoff theatre on 12th September 1996. There was no prior announcement until the audience was in. When it came you could hear the start of a sigh of disappointment because they thought Betty Buckley was indisposed.

I needn't have worried. The effusive New York audience welcomed me with an embarrassingly generous ovation. On that night that memorable first line, 'Why are you so late?!', had special meaning.

Below: Taking First Night curtain call on Broadway, Minskoff Theatre, 12th September 1996.

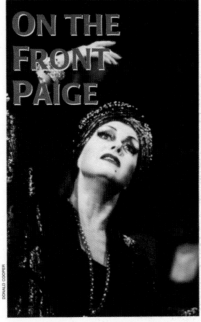

ON THE FRONT PAIGE

Photo: DONALD COOPER

Elaine Paige, London's acclaimed musical theatre star, is at last making her Broadway debut in Sunset Boulevard

MINSKOFF THEATRE

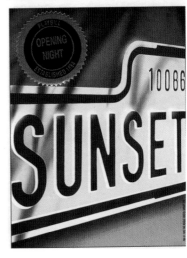

Each night, when Elaine Paige descends the mammoth staircase onstage at the Minskoff Theatre, it is the fulfillment of, if not a lifelong dream, then an 18-year one. The award-winning English actress, who created the lead roles in *Evita, Cats* and *Chess* on the London stage, had hoped with each critically lauded performance to make the transatlantic leap to her New York debut, but she was foiled each time. It's probably for this reason that during her first week in New York, the charming and youthfully exuberant Paige exclaimed: "I really can't believe I'm here! When I'm up on that stage for the first time, then I will believe it."

And what a role for a Broadway debut: Norma Desmond, the egomaniacal silent screen star of Andrew Lloyd Webber's *Sunset Boulevard,* a part that won Paige an Olivier Award nomination when she replaced another Norma Desmond legend, Betty Buckley, in the London production.

Paige first stepped into the role briefly—and on very short notice—when Buckley underwent an emergency appendectomy. Paige confesses that when she saw Glenn Close perform the role in New York, just as she was to begin her own rehearsals, she thought, "Oh yikes . . . I've only got two-and-a-half weeks [to rehearse], and this is really a massive undertaking.' I suddenly thought, 'Crikey, I don't know if I'll be able to do this.' "

Paige needn't have worried: She received glowing reviews from the London critics for her multi-textured portrayal, an interpretation that not only wrings out every ounce of dramatic action but delivers some unexpected humor as well. "[Norma] has many facets to her," Paige explains, "and I think she did have a sense of humor. I think, also, she could be very vulnerable as well as being demonstrative and overpowering, a general bossy boots, and appalling and hurtful and dreadful. There are all these elements to her, and I wanted to try to bring as much fullness to this woman."

An artist of tremendous talent, Paige's gift is to dissect a role and determine what phrasing, gesture or emotion can bring a scene to its fullest dramatic potential. Fittingly, she concedes that she is happiest during the rehearsal process when "you're experimenting; you can make a bit of a fool of yourself and nobody sees; it's being able to delve and discover."

Just watch as the diminutive powerhouse pours out her heart and voice in "As If We Never Said Goodbye," her second act show-stopper in *Sunset.* The song—set in a movie studio at Paramount, where Norma Desmond acted in the films that made her a star—is at once a recollection of Desmond's glorious past and a deluded belief that she will return to the screen.

by Andrew Gans

48

Above: Elaine Stritch, en route to perform in A Delicate Balance, *hair in rollers, visited me backstage to wish me luck for my opening night. She joked and growled at me 'You're too short to be a star!'*

Right: I joined the Hall of Fame at Sardi's Restaurant. What an honour (if a bit lopsided).

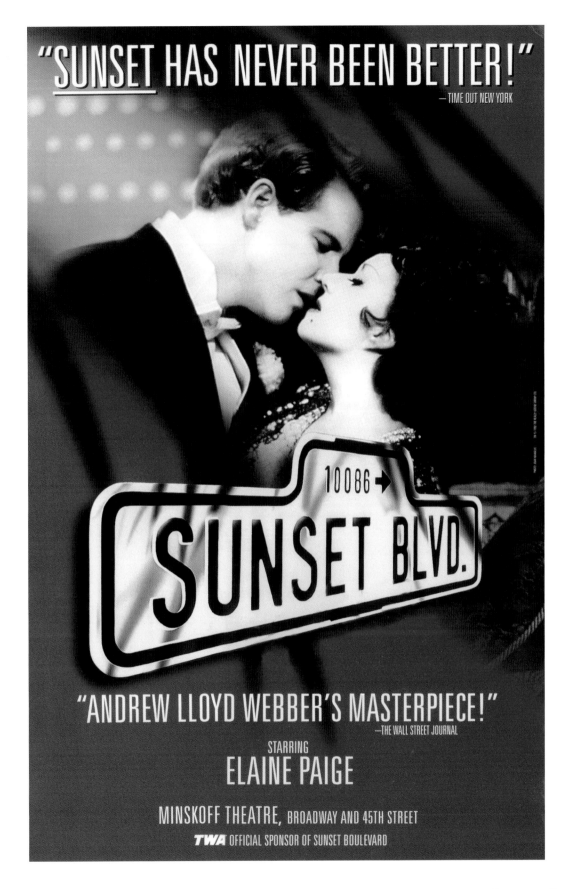

"**SUNSET** HAS NEVER BEEN BETTER!"

—TIME OUT NEW YORK

10086 →

SUNSET BLVD.

"ANDREW LLOYD WEBBER'S MASTERPIECE!"

—THE WALL STREET JOURNAL

STARRING
ELAINE PAIGE

MINSKOFF THEATRE, BROADWAY AND 45TH STREET

TWA OFFICIAL SPONSOR OF SUNSET BOULEVARD

Above: Alan Campbell and I shared a 'tipple' of Remy Martin brandy in the wings of each performance prior to the curtain call.
He was the most focused and generous of actors to work with and needless to say I fell in love with him nightly. We still share a
'tipple' or two whenever we get together.

9

The King and I

Book and Lyrics: Oscar Hammerstein II

Music: Richard Rodgers

London Palladium, 2000

Sweeney Todd

Book: Hugh Wheeler

Music and Lyrics: Stephen Sondheim

New York City Opera, 2004

The Drowsy Chaperone

Book: Bob Martin and Don McKellar

Music and Lyrics: Lisa Lambert and Greg Morrison

Novello Theatre, London, 2007

Rodgers and Hammerstein's
THE KING
and
I

LONDON PALLADIUM

TIME TO PLAY a classic American musical for a change. To explore the challenge of singing the fifth collaboration of Rodgers and Hammerstein perhaps?

The idea for their period musical set in the 1860s – based on the novel by Margaret Landon – had been suggested to them by Gertrude Lawrence who'd wanted to play the leading role of Anna Leonowens. I could see why.

Driven. That's how I describe many of the women I've played: determined and decisive. 'Mrs Anna' in *The King and I* is an intriguing character: educated, independent, unconventional and opinionated; she knew what she wanted from life and was determined to succeed against the odds, even though that meant that she had to overcome the many restrictions imposed on women in both her own society and that of King Mongkut of Siam.

I loved *The King and I* as a show: the confrontation of vastly different cultures, the experiences of this very British woman travelling halfway round the world with a young son and being exposed to the exotic world of the Siamese King with his many wives and children.

Richard Rodgers' tunes are lyrical, so I would need to use much more of my 'head' voice. A change from the middle vocal range I've been associated with in the modern musical. An entirely different approach is required: lots of breath for all those long phrases. Chris Renshaw, the director, was keen that

Below: With some of the King's children.

the music should come out of the dialogue, so we took time to set the keys so that the speech would follow on into the song seamlessly.

I agreed to play 'Mrs Anna' opposite the Tony award-winning Lou Diamond Phillips who had played the King on Broadway but rather suddenly he had to withdraw and the part was recast and given to the film actor Jason Scott Lee.

Knowing that the portrayal of the King was crucial to the show, with the balance of the play weighted towards him, I was hesitant but I had already signed the contract.

Our rehearsals began on March 6th 2000, in the appropriately titled Royal Receiving Room just off the magnificent Royal Circle Bar in the Theatre Royal Drury Lane. Chris Renshaw explained respect for Thailand (then called Siam), its architecture, its customs, its region, its people, is the order of the day for this new production. One of my favourite aspects of the rehearsal period is to research and devour all the information I can find.

The public expectation was high and £8 million had been taken at the box office before the opening night, and 'we waltzed back into the West End in triumph' (*Daily Mirror*). But in truth the critics were cool.

The first of my many Kings! Jason Scott Lee, Palladium Theatre, 2000.

Right: A first night gift from Herbert Lom to me. He had played the role of the King at Drury Lane Theatre, opening on 8 October 1953. I too wish he could have waited to be my King.

Sadly Jason had to withdraw after only three months for personal reasons; and I could never have imagined that I would still be rehearsing daily over six months later with a catalogue of Kings, and performing the arduous role every night. The nightly 64-bar polka and the large crinolines didn't help either. My dresser Spencer Kitchen and I struggled in the wings with the many layers of clothing in extreme heat. Both she and Robin Kermode, playing Sir Edward Ramsay, were a great support – Spennie continually wafting a fan under my petticoats and Robin, who I always called 'Sir', cracking brilliant jokes. But even so it took a toll on my health and I dropped two dress sizes.

I was bruised by the whole experience and it would take me some time to recover before I was able to go back on stage again, in a musical anyway. However before long, as the lyric says, you just have to 'pick yourself up, dust yourself off and start all over again'.

Sweeney Todd

I saw the Royal Opera House's version of *Sweeney Todd* on the 12th December 2003 with Thomas Allen as Sweeney and Felicity Palmer as Mrs Lovett. It began a general discussion in the UK press about what constitutes an 'opera'. Two months later I was on my way to play Mrs Lovett myself, at the New York City Opera – this powerful piece 'crossed over' and was now acknowledged by the operatic world.

Sondheim subtitled *Sweeney Todd* a 'musical thriller' and said his music had been influenced by Bernard Herrmann – the man who composed the scores of many of Hitchcock's most famous thrillers, like *North by Northwest*, *Vertigo*, and *Psycho*. It's an open secret that Sweeney is an homage to Herrmann's language which Sondheim thought had a way of making a mood of suspense. All the people in the play are driven to acts of desperation, the music is dark and full of foreboding, similar to horror movies, which makes it very scary. A melodrama.

My first scene with Sweeney, Mark Delavan. Every night before The Worst Pies in London *I would pace up and down nervously reciting the entire lyric before making my entrance. Something I've never done in any other show.*

Right: With (left to right) Mark Delavan, Hal Prince, Artie Masella and Abe Jacob.

Opposite: My first taste of Sondheim. (Please sir can I have some more?)

On 16th December, I begin learning the music under the watchful eye of my friend and Musical Director, John Owen Edwards. As is the case with the opera world, I am expected to arrive knowing the role! And just as well, because with only three weeks' rehearsal when you put *Sweeney* on its feet, with so much staging and handling of props, there's no time for worrying about the notes.

I had long wanted to sing a score by Stephen Sondheim and had always been intrigued by the complexity of Mrs Lovett's character. On the one hand, Mrs Lovett is a cheerful, chatty, cockney pie-maker, but she's also a woman without a single scruple, wiping her greasy fingers and slapping roaches off the table with inimitable flair and panache. She provides some comic relief, but it is she who also has the grisly thought in the song *A Little Priest* that 'With the price of meat what it is'…why waste the corpses Mr Todd's razor could provide?… So here are two desperate people discussing the gastronomic merits of their victims.

It was going to be a major challenge to pit myself against the trained voices of the world of opera, but one that was to be a truly rewarding experience. Probably the most difficult of any score I have sung, but with conversational lyrics full of wit and humour that lay exactly on the melody, making it a pleasure to learn and eventually perform.

The first day of rehearsal takes place at the State Theater rehearsal room and as I walk in, there stand two men: Artie Marsella, the director, and Mark Delavan, a great big bear of a man who is to play Sweeney Todd. I feel very small next to him.

The focus was almost entirely on the singing. And boy could they sing. The volume was deafening. Even though Mark was

Right: The tall and the short of it:
with Mark Delavan, my Sweeney Todd.

Below: With (left to right) Judi Dench,
Julia McKenzie, Millicent Martin,
Bernadette Peters, Stephen Sondheim
and Maria Friedman backstage during
Hey Mr Producer, *celebrating Cameron*
Mackintosh's 30th Anniversary as a
musical producer, Lyceum Theatre, 1998.

6'4" towering above me, the strength of his instrument hurt my ears! I decided I would need to change my approach so I dared to use my soprano head voice, something that I had not done in this way before. With every performance it grew stronger and with only a minimum of amplification to help us.

I felt a real sense of achievement.

We were to sing only 18 performances in repertoire with the modern opera *Mourning Becomes Electra* and Handel's *Xerxes* over a period of a month. Having several days off between each performance was new to me and that in itself became an added challenge. But the dream to be back on Broadway and to be singing a Stephen Sondheim score had been realised.

The Drowsy Chaperone

Sitting in his dowdy bed-sit apartment, 'The Man In The Chair' invites the audience to join him in his love of musical theatre and in particular in reliving one of his favourites: the (fictional) 1920s Broadway hit, *The Drowsy Chaperone*. He drops the needle onto the record and the whole show comes to life with a cast of colourful characters bursting out of his fridge. The story is simple: it centres around the nuptials of showgirl Janet van de Graff and Robert Martin and their wedding guests.

It was originally written by friends and fellow members of a Toronto-based comedy troupe for the *actual* Janet and Robert as a wedding gift. It was a 40-minute pastiche of the musicals of the 1920s in all their exuberant, gay, tap-dancing glory. After the couple had been presented with their wedding treat, Bob Martin joined his acting pals on stage and famously joked 'Well, I have some notes'. And so the musical comedy, *The Drowsy Chaperone*, was born.

Not just a pastiche or a pantomime, *The Drowsy Chaperone* was an affectionate, clever, witty and totally original look at musicals from a modern perspective. The brilliant premise of 'The Man In The Chair' commenting and being interrupted by his *modern* life works on many levels. The result is a post-modern view of the world: reality only comes into being through our interpretations of what the world means to us individually.

The conceit of *The Drowsy Chaperone* is also that the cast are playing actors playing the characters in the musical. I was Beatrice Stockwell, an elegant actress of many past triumphs, known for singing rousing ballads and here playing the title role of the 'drowsy' chaperone to Janet van de Graff. Beatrice always does her own thing and likes to 'keep her eyeball on the highball in her hand'! Great, I thought, no acting required! Just kidding!

'Girls just want to have fun' – and with such a great

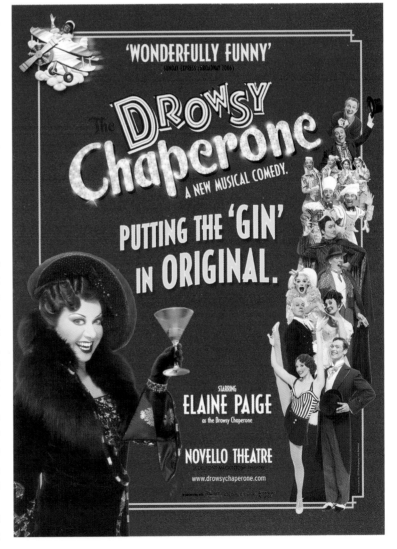

company, fun it was. One of the producers of the show, Kevin McCollum, said 'it's a bit like falling in love, it doesn't make any sense but it's completely wonderful' And he was right. Never before have I heard a British audience howl with laughter for one hour and forty minutes every night. They loved it. We thought we had a hit on our hands. But too soon the comedy turned to tragedy.

The company were called in to be given the bad news. After only two months, the show was to close. I've only once before in my career felt so upset and disappointed and shed a tear, and that was way back in the sixties at the closing of *The Roar of the Greasepaint – the Smell of the Crowd*; my first professional show. I knew that for us all to play comedy on a month's notice, wouldn't be easy. So, to boost morale, I mentioned that Stephen Sondheim's *Anyone Can Whistle*, a musical now regarded as a classic, closed after just nine performances. At least we made nine weeks.

I am still often asked today, 'What happened to *The Drowsy Chaperone*?', 'Why did it close?' I wish I knew the answer.

Opposite, top: As Beatrice Stockwell, the Drowsy Chaperone, making her entrance through the Man In The Chair's fridge.

Opposite, bottom: With Nickolas Grace as Underling, the butler, trying to get the vodka gag right – this was the fourth version and the one the audience loved, so we played it to the hilt!

Above: With Joseph Alessi as the outrageous lothario, Aldolpho, who tried everything in the book to seduce me.

Left: Beatrice is in a straitjacket, but still with a drink in her hand.

Above: A tête à tête with Anna Carteret in The Misanthrope.

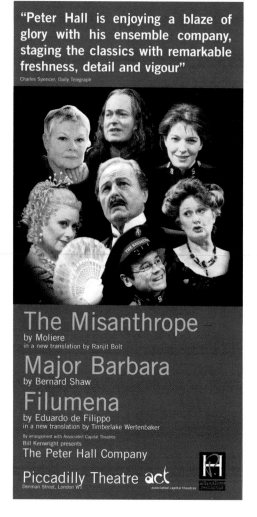

"Peter Hall is enjoying a blaze of glory with his ensemble company, staging the classics with remarkable freshness, detail and vigour"

Charles Spencer, Daily Telegraph

The Misanthrope
by Moliere
in a new translation by Ranjit Bolt

Major Barbara
by Bernard Shaw

Filumena
by Eduardo de Filippo
in a new translation by Timberlake Wertenbaker

By arrangement with Associated Capital Theatres
Bill Kenwright presents
The Peter Hall Company

Piccadilly Theatre act
Denman Street, London W1   associated capital theatres

Since working with Peter Hall on Piaf, *he has given me the opportunity to act in his renowned Peter Hall Company. He cast me as Célimène in Molière's* The Misanthrope *alongside classical heavyweights Michael Pennington, David Yelland, Peter Bowles, and Anna Carteret. We played in repertoire with* Waiting for Godot, Filumena *and* Major Barbara *at the Piccadilly Theatre, London, for six weeks in 1998. I missed hearing the overture each night but speaking the verse was like singing the song without music. A challenge for sure, but surrounded by such illustrious company, it's one I relished.*

In 2003 Peter asked me to join the company again to play Angèle in a new adaptation of Feydeau's farce Le système ribadier, *entitled* Where There's a Will, *this time with classical actors David Warner (below left), Nicholas Le Prevost (below right) and David Bamber. Edith Piaf used to say that she had always worked with the best people and I remembered thinking that I have been lucky enough to do the same. The portrait (above right) is by Louise Riley-Smith: it was shortlisted for the Garrick Milne Prize.*

10

Another Suitcase in Another Hall

IT'S FUNNY how things have a way of turning up unexpectedly, and the offer to host a weekly programme for BBC Radio Two came along just at the right time, giving me a new direction.

I met with Malcolm Prince, my producer, with whom I immediately hit it off. We had a natural rapport and I knew he'd be great fun to work with and I would be able to rely on his considerable experience. We discussed the possible content of the programme and since there wasn't one devoted to musical theatre, a subject I knew a bit about, we decided that that was the route to go.

And so *Elaine Paige on Sunday*, *E.P.O.S.*, began.

Unlike theatre, radio is an intimate medium, a one-to-one scenario, involving reaching people in their sitting rooms, their cars, on the train. I love the dialogue with the audience: they tell me their likes and dislikes. It's direct contact, just like a friendship. My programme has given me the chance to make new friends and reacquaint myself with old ones. It has also given me

Below: With my Radio producer Malcolm Prince.

the opportunity to interview some fascinating people, allowing both the audience and myself to discover more about their lives, careers and favourite musicals.

How can I forget, for example, having tea with Angela Lansbury and discussing such 'Essential Musicals' as *Gypsy*, *Mame* and *Sweeney Todd* (the latter something we have in common)? Or talking about Vincente Minnelli and Judy Garland with their daughter Liza? Or learning how Elton John and Tim Rice helped to create *The Lion King*? It's quite an education. (And all this without having to worry about hair and make-up!)

As radio continues to evolve, the show has become even more accessible: with websites, the BBC iPlayer and podcasts making it possible to hear any programme at any time, anywhere in the world, including *E.P.O.S.*!

The response has been amazing and the public have really embraced it. What Malcolm and I envisaged as a show for devotees of the genre was actually the catalyst for a resurgence of a national interest in musical theatre. You could say *E.P.O.S.* has helped to make musicals 'cool' again. As Elton, Johnny Mathis, Burt Bacharach, the Pet Shop Boys and Barry Manilow all told me, musical theatre plays an essential part in anyone's musical education.

But, for me, the added bonus of hosting this show is that it's tremendous fun. Only the other

Sunday, in the middle of the programme, I was reading one of the many hundreds of emails we receive every week from around the world in the *Break-a-Leg* slot. I came upon an am-dram show called *The Big Blow* which really cracked me up. So much so, I completely lost the plot and broke down with hysterical laughter. (As I'm told by my audience, this has become known as the 'EP giggle'.) To make matters worse, the following message was about a musical comedy loosely based on *Romeo and Juliet*, to be performed on Guildford High Street. Malcolm shouted, 'That's a tragedy isn't it?' I replied, 'Yes. But if you live there, it's on the street where you live!' Now Malcolm lost it and the pair of us were helpless with hilarious laughter. Cue music! OK, you had to be there. But it represents just one of the many amusing moments that take place every week.

For me, being involved in radio feels like another milestone; it's been a wonderfully liberating experience. After years of theatre and immersing myself in character, I've discovered my own voice – who *I* am. And it's interesting to realise that more people listen to the programme on a Sunday than would see a West End show in the course of a year. Yikes!

Left: With Elton John in Las Vegas following an interview for my Radio programme, 2005.

In Concert

Above: At the White House, 1988. With (left to right) Bea Arthur, Mary Martin, Nancy Reagan, President Reagan, Dorothy Loudon, Jennifer Holliday and Marvin Hamlisch.

One of my great pleasures now is to perform in concert. I wouldn't have said that in 1985 on my first solo tour. It was a daunting prospect to stand on stage alone.

But an invitation from Marvin Hamlisch to sing at the White House in 1988 toward the end of the Reagan Era was something I couldn't turn down. Not a solo concert, but still quite intimidating. Called *Showstoppers*, it was a celebration of American Musical Theatre, to be sung by the Great Ladies of the Broadway Stage: Mary Martin, Bea Arthur, Dorothy Loudon, Jennifer Holliday with Marvin accompanying on piano. Marvin had asked me to be part of this theatrical event to herald the British contingent. So there I was flying the flag at 1600 Pennsylvania Avenue, Washington DC!

I was absolutely thrilled to make my American début at such a prestigious location. I was asked specifically to sing *Don't Cry for Me Argentina* from *Evita* and *Memory* from *Cats*.

It was an honour to sing for the President and the First Lady and to be presented to them after the performance remains a great memory (excuse the pun) and a highlight in my concert career.

Performing at the White House, however, taught me an important lesson about preparation for international concert-work. I learned how necessary it is to fly to the city several days in advance to give sufficient time to recover from the predictable jetlag. Experts advise that a day is needed for each time zone travelled. Employing this well-learnt lesson I have found it to be absolutely true and accurate.

Below: I joined Marvin Hamlisch as his guest artist at the Royal Festival Hall in 1980 – my first concert performance. With my family afterwards. Happy relief.

Above: Partying following my concert performance at the London Palladium, 6th December 1987, with (left to right) Peter Straker (just!), Anita Dobson, Carol Woods and Freddie Mercury.

I've travelled internationally and sung in some of the great concert halls of the world: the Royal Albert Hall, Sydney Opera House the Abravenel Hall, Salt Lake (for the 2002 Winter Olympics); the Bolshoi Theatre in Moscow, along with the concert halls of Scandinavia as well as The Royal Opera House here in London. Like theatre, for it to work, concerts are all about team-work and getting the right creative and technical people together. I am currently working on my 40th Anniversary celebratory concerts with director Christopher Luscombe and musical director Chris Egan. You can't achieve anything on your own, you really have to have the best people around you and I've always made sure to surround myself with those who are at the top of their field. If all the elements are in place, then I can really enjoy myself out there 'on my own'.

Another landmark performance was in 2001 when I joined Kris Phillips (Fei Xiang) – the Taiwanese American popstar – in a ground-breaking concert at The Great Hall of the People in Beijing. It was ground-breaking in the sense that it was the first time that the music of Andrew Lloyd Webber or any modern western musical theatre work had been performed in China. Kris, a big star there, and I headed the company, singing highlights from Andrew's repertoire. The event was recorded for a DVD entitled *Masterpiece*.

We had been told to expect a reserved response from the audience as they knew little of the music, but on the contrary, the whole place became a riot of sound: in response to this new musical form, never before seen 'live', they applauded, they stamped their feet, and banged desk-tops (the audience sat at desks as this is a political building, not a formal concert hall). This truly was 'new territory' for us all and since then I have returned to China with my own one-woman show. As everything there continues to change at breakneck speed, audiences devour western musical theatre: like children in a sweet shop, they can't get enough. It's fantastic to be at the forefront of this exciting time in Chinese cultural history.

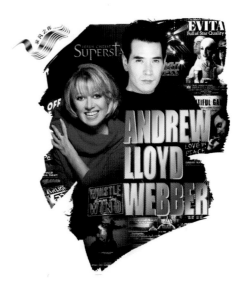

Above: The poster for the Andrew Lloyd Webber concert at The Great Hall of the People in Beijing, 2001.

Above: With Sandy Lam, Tony Vincent, Andrew Lloyd Webber and Kris Phillips (Fei Xiang) at The Great Hall of the People in Beijing, 2001. Andrew flew over especially for this momentous event, making a speech at the end of the performance, thanking the Chinese audience.

Above: With (left to right) Max Hole, MD of WEA records, Tony Visconti my record producer and Rob Dickins, Chairman of Warner. The record company Warner Bros presented us all with platinum discs for achieving 300,000 sales for my first theatre album Stages *in 1983.*

Above: Two record producers come together in 1996: Tony Visconti and Dennis Lambert celebrating in New York, the honour HMV bestowed on me – a lifetime achievement award. I thought you had to be dead to get one of those!

Above: 1993 – a recording session at CTS Studios, Wembley, with one of the all time great arrangers, Peter Matz, The Romance and the Stage *Album.*

Above: With Peter at the piano.

Above: With Mike Moran in Montreux, my MD and producer of many of my albums including one of my favourites, The Queen Album, *1988. It was the first time anyone had covered Queen's material and it was recorded with a Symphony Orchestra.*

Above: With Freddy Mercury in Montreux.

Above: At Montreux, the girl with the boys in the band, 'Queen' that is.

11

'EP'logue

SO HERE I AM celebrating forty years in the theatre.

It's been a long love affair.

My work has been the driving force in my life and though there are things I've missed in my personal life, it's been an affair of the heart.

Everything has taken a lot of hard work, drive and energy to achieve, and nothing worth having has ever come easily. I was always taught to apply oneself and I have with grit and determination. As Bette Davis said 'No guts, no glory'. But one always needs a little luck and a lot of help from others.

I've worked with so many talented people, some of the very best. What a privilege – and what a laugh we've had along the way. Fortunately, I've made many good friends who have supported and

encouraged me and whom I love and cherish. Perhaps if I ever get around to writing an autobiography, I can talk of them, my life and feelings, in more detail.

But for now, this incredible journey has taken me down many roads, and in many different directions.

I have always loved diversity and made an effort to try different things to challenge myself. I have played some incredible women, some feisty and determined, some not. I have enjoyed every one and some have worked out better than others. To have had the opportunity to be allowed to do something I love is more than I could have ever hoped for.

So from my first inspiration, hearing a recording of *West Side Story* in the Prefect's Common Room at school, 40 years on, to paraphrase the lyric of *As We Stumble Along* in *The Drowsy Chaperone*, I hope I can continue, like the character Beatrice, to:

> 'Stumble along on life's funny journey'… 'Stumble along, into the blue'

doing my own thing and 'keeping my eyeball on the' occasional 'highball in my hand'.

> 'Still I'll bumble my way through life's crazy labyrinth'

in much the same way…

> 'And the best that I can do is hope a bluebird will sing his song
> As I stumble, bumble, fumble, tumble, as I stumble along'…

Yes 'life is a whirlwind' and it passes by too fast. I hope this book with some of my 'memories' brings back a few good ones of your own.

Production Credits

Hair

Shaftesbury Avenue Theatre, London
27 September 1968

Creatives
Books and Lyrics: Gerome Ragni and
  James Rado
Music: Galt MacDermot
Produced by: Robert Stigwood
  Organisation
Executive producer: Bertrand Castelli
Dance Director: Julie Arenal
Assistant to director: David Toguri
Musical director: Derek Wadsworth
Costumes Nancy Potts
Scenery: Robin Wagner (re-created
  by Herbert Sidon)
Lighting: Jules Fisher
Sound: Robert Calder
Director: Tom O'Horan

Main cast
Claude : Paul Nicholas
Vince: J Vincent Edward
Berger: Oliver Tobias
Sheila: Annabel Leventon
with: Ena Cabayo, Ethel Coley, Tim
  Curry, Linbert Spencer, Kookie Eaton,
  Lucy Fenwick, Gary Hamilton, Linda
  Kendrick, Sonja Kristina, Peter Oliver,
  Elaine Paige, Peter Straker, Liz White

Maybe That's Your Problem

The Roundhouse, London
16th June 1971

Creatives
Original story and book:
  Lionel Chetwynd
Lyrics: Don Black
Music: Walter Scharf
Produced by: Andrew Mann
(A Raspberry Enterprises production)
Musical numbers staged and
  choreographed by: Virginia Mason
Music arranged by: John Cameron
Designed and lit by: Barrie Lowe

Cast
Marvin: Douglas Lambert
Lynn: Andee Silver
Lenny: Al Mancini
Dr Schlossman: Harold Kasket
Brenda: Liz Whiting
Andre: Basil Patton
Eadie: Elaine Paige
Ellie: Liz Whiting
Mr Gold: David Fennell
Mrs Gold: Gloria Chetwynd
Bobby: Leslie Meadows
Grandfather: Barry Lines
Mr Berkovitch: Alan Angel
Mrs Berkovitch: Christina Avery
Stein: Gloria Chetwynd
Cop: David Fennel

Jesus Christ Superstar

Palace Theatre, London
9 August 1972

Creatives
Lyrics Tim Rice
Music: Andrew Lloyd Webber
Executive Producer: Bob Walsh
Scenic Designs: Brian Thomson
Costumes: Gabriella Falk
Lighting: Jules Fisher
Musical Director: Anthony Bowles
Orchestrations: Andrew Lloyd Webber
Sound: David Collison
Movement Consultant: Rufus Collins
Director: Jim Sharman

Main cast
Jesus: Paul Nicholas
Herod: Victor Spinetti
Mary Magdalene: Dana Gillespie
Judas Iscariot: Stephen Tate
Caiaphas: George Harris
Pontius Pilate: John Parker
Simon: Derek James

Rock Carmen

The Roundhouse, London
1972

Creatives
Adapted from Bizet's and Merimée's
  Carmen
Book and Lyrics: Herb Hendler
Music: Michael Hughes
Lighting and sets by: Joe's Lights
Musical Direction by: John Hawkins and
  Jonathan Cohen
Costumes designed by: Michele Deliss
Additional songs by Herb Hendler and
  John Hawkins
Production directed and choreographed
  by: Irving Davies

Cast
Carmen: Terri Stevens
Joe: Davy Clinton
Ed: Robert Coleby
Michelle: Elaine Paige
with: Frank Aiello, Helen Gill,
  Sharon Lyle, Peter Oliver,
  Caroline Villiers, Beverley Baxter,
  Sandy Grant, Leonard Bickley,
  Peter Seargeant, Natalie Shaw

Nuts

Theatre Royal Stratford East
20 June 1973

Creatives
Devised and directed by:
  Joan Littlewood.
Musical director: Ian Armit
Costumes: Willie Burt and Sarah
  Hodgkinson
Production Manager: Mark Pritchard

Cast
Kent Baker
Larry Dann
Ken Hill
Jenny Logan
Elaine Paige
Brian Protheroe
Peter Rankin
Trevor T Smith
Bill Wallis

Grease

New London Theatre
26 June 1973

Creatives
Book, Lyrics and Music by: Jim Jacobs
  and Warren Casey
Produced by: Paul Elliot and
  Duncan C Weldon for Triumph
  Theatre Productions in association
  with Donals Langdon for Heindale by
  arrangement with Kenneth Waissman
  and Maxine Fox in association with
  Anthony D'Amato
Musical supervision and Vocal and
  Dance arrangements: Louis St Louis
Musical Direction: Barry Booth
Orchestrations: Michael Leonard
Scenery: Douglas E Schmidt
Costumes: Carrie F Robbins
Lighting: Robert Ornbo
Sound: David Collision
Directed by Tom Moore

Main cast
Sandy: Elaine Paige
Danny: Paul Nicholas

Billy

Theatre Royal Drury Lane, London
1 May 1974

Creatives
Book: Dick Clement and Ian La
  Frenais, based on *Billy Liar* by Keith
  Waterhouse and Willis Hall
Lyrics: Don Black
Music: John Barry
Produced by: Peter Witt Productions
Production design: Ralph Koltai
Costumes: Annena Stubbs
Lighting: Jules Fisher
Additional costumes: Marilyn Taylor
Sound: David Fisher and Anthony
  Taylor
Vocal and dance arrangements: Ray
  Holder
Music arranged and orchestrated by:
  John Barry and Bobby Richards
Director: Patrick Garland

Cast
Billy: Michael Crawford
Mrs Fisher: Avis Bunnage
Shadrack: Christopher Hancock
Barbara: Gay Soper
Rita: Elaine Paige
Mr Fisher: Bryan Pringle
Arthur: Billy Boyle
Stamp: Barry James
Duxbury: Lockwood West
Liz: Diana Quick
Gran Fisher: Betty Turner
Mrs Crabtree: Elsie Wilson

The Boyfriend

Haymarket Theatre, Leicester
11 November 1976

Creatives
Book, Lyrics and Music: Sandy Wilson
Designer: Clive Lavagna
Musical Director: Robert Mandell
Associate Musical Director: Ian Smith
Choreographer: David Thornton
Lighting: Chris Ellis
Sound: Rod Mead
Director: Alexander Dore

Cast
Hortense: Mia Nadasi
Maisie: Elaine Paige
Dulcie: Jacqueline Redden
Fay: Belinda Lang
Nancy: Sara Pugsley
Polly Browne: Amy Nissen
Marcel: David Timson
Pierre: Jim Hooper
Alphonse: Crispin Thomas
Madame Dubonnet: Miriam Karlin
Bobby Van Husen: Martin Smith
Percival Browne: Darryle Kavann
Tony: John Conroy
Lord Brockhurst: Alexander Dore
Lady Brockhurst: Grania Hayes

Evita

Prince Edward Theatre, London
21 June 1978

Creatives
Lyrics: Tim Rice
Music: Andrew Lloyd Webber
Produced by: Robert Stigwood in
    association with David Land
Executive producer: Bob Swash
Lighting: David Hersey
Sound: Abe Jacob
Musical directors: Anthony Bowles
Orchestrations: Hersay Kay
Original orchestrations and vocal
    arrangements by: Andrew Lloyd
    Webber.
Designed by: Timothy O'Brien and
    Tazeena Firth
Choreography: Larry Fuller
Director: Harold Prince

Cast
Che: David Essex
Evita: Elaine Paige
Peron: Joss Ackland
The Mistress: Siobhan McCarthy
Magaldi: Mark Ryan

Cats

New London Theatre
11 May 1981

Creatives
Book: Based on *Old Possum's Book of
    Practical Cats* by T S Eliot
Lyrics: T S Eliot
Additional Lyrics by: Don Black and
    Trevor Nunn
Music: Andrew Lloyd Webber

Produced by: Cameron Mackintosh and
    The Really Useful Company Ltd
Orchestrations: Andrew Lloyd Webber
    and David Cullen
Musical director: Harry Rabinowitz
Sound: Abe Jacob
Lighting By David Hersey
Designed by John Napier
Associate director and choreographer:
    Gillian Lynne
Director: Trevor Nunn

Cast
Rum Tum Tugger: Paul Nicholas
Old Deuteronomy / Bustopher Jones:
    Brian Blessed
Mistoffelees: Wayne Sleep
Grizabella: Elaine Paige
Alonzo: Ronald Alexander
Carbucketty: David Baxter
Jemima: Sarah Brightman
George: John Chester
Bombalurina: Geraldine Gardner
Victoria: Finola Hughes
Cassandra: Seeta Indrani
Demeter: Sharon Lee-Hill
Jennyanydots: Myra Sands
Munkustrap: Jeff Shankley
Jellylorum / Griddlebone: Susan Jane
    Tanner
Gus the Theatre Cat / Growltiger:
    Stephen Tate
Tantomile: Femi Taylor
Mungojerrie: John Thornton
Rumpelteazer: Bonnie Langford
Coricopat: Donald Waugh
Skimbleshanks: Ken Wells
The Kittens: Peter Barry, Julie Edmett,
    Anita Pashley, Stephen Wayne
The Cats Chorus: Jeni Evans, Nick
    Hamilton, Stephen Hill, Nicola Kimber

Abbacadabra

The Lyric Theatre, Hammersmith
8 December 1983

Creatives
Book: David Wood
Original story by: Alain and
  Daniel Boublil
Lyrics: Don Black Additional Lyrics:
  Mike Batt and Björn Ulvaeus
Music by: Abba (Björn Ulvaeus and
  Benny Andersson)
Produced by: The Lyric Theatre,
  Hammersmith by arrangement with
  Cameron Mackintosh
Music staging and choreography:
  Anthony van Laast
Set Design: Jenny Tiramani
Costume: Sue Blane
Lighting: Andrew Bridge
Sound Design: Andrew Bruce for
  Autograph sound
Orchestrations: David Cullen
Additional Orchestrations: Mike Batt
Musical Direction: Simon Webb
Director: Peter James

Cast
Miss Williams/Carabosse: Elaine Paige
Linda: Jenna Russell
Peter: Nigel Harman/Richard Hagon
John: Dexter Fletcher
Cinderella: Finola Hughes
Aladdin: Michael Praed
Pinocchio: Sylvester McCoy
Beast: B A Robertson
Fred: Phil Daniels
Joe Crow: Claude Paul Henry
Zeke Beak: Stewart Avon Arnold
Supercrow: Geoff David
Flo Crow: Linda-Mae Brewer
Sleeping Beauty: Jayne Leigh Collins

Chess

Prince Edward Theatre, London
14 May 1986

Creatives
Lyrics: Tim Rice
Music: Björn Ulvaeus and
  Benny Andersson
Produced by: 3 Knights Ltd, The Shubert
  Organisation, Robert Fox Ltd for Chess
  Productions Ltd
Scene Design: Robin Wagner
Costume design: Theoni V Alderidge
Lighting design: David Hersey
Orchestrations and arrangements:
  Anders Eljas
Sound design: Andrew Bruce
Executive producers: Judy Craymer and
  Tyler Gatchell
Musical direction: John Owen Edwards
Choreography: Molly Molloy
Director: Trevor Nunn

Cast
Mayor of Merano: Richard Mitchell
Frederick Trumper: Murray Head
Florence Vassey: Elaine Paige
Alexander Molokov: John Turner
Anatoly Sergievsky: Tommy Körberg
Walter de Courcey: Kevin Colson
The Arbiter: Tom Jobe
Principal TV Presenter: Peter Karrie
Civil servants: Richard Lyndon and Paul
  Wilson
Svetlana Sergievsky: Siobhan McCarthy

Anything Goes

Prince Edward Theatre, London
4 July 1989

Creatives
Original Book: P G Wodehouse &
Guy Bolton, and Howard Lindsay &
Russel Crouse
New Book: Timothy Crouse and
John Weidman
Music and Lyrics: Cole Porter (1934)
Produced by: Robert Fox Ltd, Anchorage
  Productions Ltd & Joan and Joe
  Cullman presented the Lincoln Center
  Theatre Production
Choreographed: Michael Smuin
Sound: Tony Meola for Autograph
Assistant to Choreographer: Kirk
  Peterson
Poster Art: James McMullan
Musical Director: John Owen Edwards
Orchestrations: Michael Gibson
Dance arrangements: Tom Fay
Lighting: Paul Gallo
Setting and costumes: Tony Walton.
Director: Jerry Zaks

Cast
Reno Sweeney: Elaine Paige
Moonface Martin: Bernard Cribbins
Billy Crocker: Howard McGillin (then
  John Barrowman)
Elisha Whitney: Harry Towb
Erma: Kathryn Evans
Mrs Evangeline Harcourt: Ursula Smith
Lord Evelyn Oakleigh: Martin Turner
Hope Harcourt: Ashleigh Sendin
Captain: David Bacon
The Purser: David Bexon
Luke: Hi Ching
John: John Smith
Fred: Nigel Waugh
Young Girl: Anita Pashley

Sailor: Anthony Lyn
Purity: Jacqui Boatswain
Chastity: Sarah Drummond
Charity: Nicola Meerloo
Virtue: Suzanne Maria Thomas
Minister: Brian Ellis
Mrs Wentworth Frick: June Bland

Piaf

Thorndike Theatre, Leatherhead
22 September 1993 and on tour
Piccadilly Theatre, London
13 December 1993

Creatives
Written by: Pam Gems
Produced by: Bill Kenwright presenting
  The Peter Hall Company
Designer: John Gunter
Lighting designer: David Hersey
Sound designer: Paul Arditti
Musical director: Laurie Holloway
Assistant director: John Bashford
Director: Peter Hall

Cast
Piaf: Elaine Paige
with Wendy Morgan, Polly Kemp, Dawn
  Hope, Lorren Bent, Ron Emslie, Rocky
  Marshall, Joe Jones, John Arthur,
  Michael Roberts, Stephen Noonan,
  Steven Serlin, Andrew Vezey and Greg
  Hicks
Understudy: Lorraine Brunning

Sunset Boulevard

Adelphi Theatre, London
29 November 1994
Minskoff Theatre, New York
12 September 1996

Creatives
Book and Lyrics: Don Black and
  Christopher Hampton, based on the
  screenplay by Billy Wilder and Charles
  Brackett and D M Marshman Jr
Music: Andrew Lloyd Webber
Produced by: The Really Useful Co Ltd
  and Paramount Pictures
Production designed by: John Napier
Costumes designed by: Anthony Powell
Lighting designed by: Andrew Bridge
Musical supervision and direction:
  David Caddick
Sound designed by Martin Levan
Musical Director: David White
Resident director: Andrew MacBean
Orchestrations by David Cullen and
  Andrew Lloyd Webber
Musical staging: Bob Avian
Director: Trevor Nunn

Main cast (London)
Norma Desmond: Elaine Paige
Joe Gillis: John Barrowman
Max von Mayerling: Michael Bauer
Betty Schaefer: Catherine Porter

Main cast (Broadway)
Norma Desmond: Elaine Paige
Joe Gillis: Alan Campbell
Max von Mayerling: George Hearn
Betty Schaefer: Alice Ripley

The Misanthrope

Piccadilly Theatre, London
26 March 1998

Creatives
Written by: Molière
Translator: Ranjit Bolt
Produced by: Bill Kenwright presenting
  the Peter Hall Company
Designer: John Gunter
Director: Peter Hall

Cast
Alceste: Michael Pennington
Philinte: David Yelland
Oronte: Peter Bowles
Célimène: Elaine Paige
Basque: Dickon Tyrrell
Eliante: Rebecca Saire
Clitandre: Crispin Bonham-Carter
Acaste: John Elmes
An Officer of the Marshalls of France /
  Du Bois: Stephen Noonan
Arsinoé: Anna Carteret

The King and I

London Palladium
3 May 2000

Creatives
Book: Oscar Hammerstein II, based on
  the novel by Margaret Langdon
Lyrics: Oscar Hammerstein II
Music: Richard Rodgers
Produced by: SEL and GFO, David Ian
  Productions Ltd, Dodger Theatrical
  Holdings Inc in association with
  The Rodgers and Hammerstein
  Organization
Scene design: Brian Thompson
Costume Design: Roger Kirk
Lighting design: Nigel Levings
Musical supervision and direction: John
  Owen Edwards
Sound Design: Paul Groothuis
Orchestration: Robert Russell Bennett
Additional Orchestrations:
  Bruce Coughlin
Musical staging: Lar Lubovitch
Choreography: Jerome Robbins
Director: Christopher Renshaw

Cast
Anna Leonowens: Elaine Paige
King of Siam: Jason Scott Lee
with: Richard Avery, Christopher
  Hawkins / Benjamin Ibbott, Miguel
  Diaz, Ho Yi, Sean Ghazi, Aura Deva,
  Taewon Yi Kim, Alexander Deng /
  Joseph Tadiar, Jeana Leah Cachero,
  Charlotte Nguyen, Robin Kermode

Where There's a Will

Yvonne Arnaud Theatre, Guildford
and tour
29 April 2003

Creatives
Written by: Georges Feydeau
Translator: Nicki Frei
Produced by: Theatre Royal Bath
  Productions presenting The Peter Hall
  Company
Designed by: Ti Green
Director: Peter Hall

Cast
Ribadier: Nicholas Le Prevost
Angèle: Elaine Paige
Thommereux : David Warner
Savinet: David Bamber

Sweeney Todd

New York City Opera
9 March 2004

Creatives

Book: Hugh Wheeler, from an
  adaptation by Christopher Bond
Music and Lyrics: Stephen Sondheim
Produced by: New York City Opera
Original Director: Harold Prince
Orchestrations by: Jonathan Tunick
Production: Harold Prince
Stage Director: Arthur Masella

Cast

Sweeney Todd: Mark Delavan
Mrs Lovett: Elaine Paige
with Judith Blazer, Keith Phares,
  Walter Charles, Roland Rusinek,
  Sarah Coburn, Keith Jameson,
  Andrew Drost, William Ledbetter

The Drowsy Chaperone

Novello Theatre, London
14 May 2007

Creatives

Book: Bob Martin and Don McKellar
Music and Lyrics: Lisa Lambert and
  Greg Morrison
Produced by: Kevin McCollum, Roy
  Miller, Bob Boyett, Stephanie P
  McClelland, Barbara Heller Freitag,
  Jill Furman
Scenic design: David Gallo
Costume: Gregg Barnes
Lighting design: Ken Billington and
  Brian Monahan
Sound design: Acme Sound Partners
Casting: Pippa Ailion
Choreographed and directed by:
  Casey Nicholaw

Cast

The Man In The Chair: Bob Martin
  (then Steve Pemberton)
The Drowsy Chaperone: Elaine Paige
Janet van de Graaff: Summer Strallen
Aldolpho: Joseph Alessi
Underling: Nickolas Grace
Robert Martin: John Partridge
Kitty: Selina Chilton
Trix: Enyonam Gbesmete
Gangster: Cameron Jack
Gangster: Adam Stafford
Tottendale: Anne Rogers
George: Sean Kingsley
with: Nina French, Mark Goldthorp,
  Paul Iveson, Sherrie Pennington,
  Kenneth Avery-Clark, Vanessa Barmby,
  Chris Bennett, Vivienne Carlyle,
  Mark Dickinson, Lincoln Stone

Photograph Credits

Oberon Books would like to thank the following for their kind permission to reproduce the images in this book. Any photograph not referred to is in the author's collection. Every effort has been made to trace and contact the photographers and copyright holders.

7: Richard Young / Rex Features

16: Unknown

19 (Bottom): Unknown

22 (Top): Michael Butler

22 (Bottom right): Robert Hirst Studios

23: Robert Hirst Studios

24 (Bottom): Unknown

25: Unknown

28: Design: Dewynters Ltd London. © Really Useful Theatre Group Ltd

29: John Haynes (www.johnhaynesphotography.com)

30 (Top): Theatre Royal Stratford East. Cartoon by Larry (Terence Parkes)

30 (Bottom): Theatre Royal Stratford East

31 (Top): Paul Elliott Ltd

31 (Bottom): Unknown

32 (Top): Unknown

32 (Bottom): Hulton Archive / Getty Images

33 (Top): Unknown

33 (Bottom): Zoë Dominic

34: Zoë Dominic

35 (Top): Zoë Dominic

35 (Bottom): Zoë Dominic

35 (Bottom): Zoë Dominic

36 (Top): Unknown

36 (Bottom): Express Syndication

37: Express Syndication

38 (Top): Unknown

38 (Bottom right): Unknown

38 (Bottom left): Unknown

39 (Top): Unknown

39 (Bottom): Unknown

42: Poster design: Dewynters Ltd London. © Dewynters Ltd London

43: Zoë Dominic

44: Unknown

45 (Top): Unknown

45 (Bottom): Zoë Dominic

46 (Top): John Timbers

46 (Bottom left): Sunday Times Magazine / NI Syndication

46 (Bottom right): Design: Dewynters Ltd London

47 (Top): Solo Syndication / Associated Newspapers

47 (Bottom): John Timbers

48, 49 Madame Tussauds

50: Zoë Dominic

51: (Top): Zoë Dominic

51: (Bottom left): Nobby Clark

51 (Bottom right): Zoë Dominic

52: Zoë Dominic

53 (Top): Zoë Dominic

53 (Bottom): Zoë Dominic

54 (Top): Zoë Dominic

54 (Bottom): Zoë Dominic

55 (Top): Zoë Dominic

55 (Bottom): Zoë Dominic

56 (Top): United Press International

56 (Bottom): Paul Smith

57: Design: Dewynters, © Really Useful Theatre Group Ltd

58 (Top): Solo Syndication / Associated Newspapers

58 (Bottom): Unknown

59 (Top): Solo Syndication/ Associated Newspapers Ltd

59 (Bottom): Mirrorpix

60 (Top left): Unknown

60 (Top right): Paul Smith

60 (Bottom): Paul Smith

62 (Top): Doug McKenzie

62 (Bottom): Doug McKenzie

63 (Bottom): BBC

63 (Bottom): Doug McKenzie

66 (Top): Poster Design: Dewynters Ltd London. © Really Useful Theatre Group Ltd and Cameron Mackintosh Ltd

66 (Bottom): Alan Davidson

67: PA Photos

68 (Top): Really Useful Group Ltd

68 (Bottom): Geoff Dixon

69: Michael Le Poer Trench

70 (Top left): Unknown

70 (Top right): Unknown

71: Unknown

72 (Top right): London Express News Service

72 (Top left): Design by Dewynters Ltd London. © Cameron Mackintosh Ltd

72 (Bottom): Jerome Yates

73 (Top): Designed by Dewynters Ltd London. © Cameron Mackintosh Ltd

73 (Bottom): Andre Csillag / Rex Features

74 (Top): ITV Granada

74 (Bottom): ITV Granada

75 (Top): Brent Walker TV productions Ltd

75 (Bottom): Brent Walker TV productions Ltd

78 (Top): Poster Design: Dewynters Ltd London. © Robert Fox Ltd

78 (Bottom): Alan Davidson

79 (Top): Unknown

79 (Bottom): Cameron Mackintosh Ltd

80 (Top): Michael Le Poer Trench

80 (Bottom): Unknown

81: Michael Le Poer Trench

82 (Bottom): Unknown

83: David Montgomery

84: Unknown

85: Unknown

86: PA Photos

87 (Top): Image by Jim McMullan used on the poster of *Anything Goes*, originally produced by Lincoln Center Theater, prior to 1989, and brought over to London, England, 1989.

87 (Bottom): Solo Syndication / Associated Newspapers

88 (Bottom): Anthony Crickmay, Camera Press London

89 (Top): Anthony Crickmay , Camera Press London

90: The Estate of William Hewison

91: PA Photos

92: Tony Walton

93: Anthony Crickmay, Camera Press London

94 (Top): BBC

94 (Bottom): BBC

95 (Top): BBC

95 (Bottom): ITV / Rex Features

98: Poster design: Dewynters Ltd London. Photograph: Anthony Crickmay, Camera Press London

99: Unknown

100: Express Syndication

104 (Top): Unknown

105: Unknown

110: Poster design; Dewynters Ltd London. © Dewynters Ltd London

111: Donald Cooper

112 (Top left): Anthony Powell

112 (Top right): Donald Cooper

113 (Top): Donald Cooper

113 (Bottom): Richard Young / Rex features

114 (Top): Richard Young / Rex Features

115: Richard Young / Rex features

116 (Top): Richard Young / Rex features

116 (Bottom): Richard Young / Rex features

117 (Centre): Unknown

117 (Bottom left): Unknown

117 (Bottom right): Unknown

118 (Top): Richard Young / Rex Features

119: Poster design: Dewynters London, Ltd © Really Useful Group Theatre Ltd

122 (Top): Original artwork by Doug Johnson

122 (Bottom): Michael Le Poer Trench

123: Michael Le Poer Trench

124: John Vickers

125: From the NYCO production of *Sweeney Todd* © Carol Rosegg

127: From the NYCO production of *Sweeney Todd* © Carol Rosegg

128 (Bottom): Unknown

129: Adam Kenwright Associates

130 (Top): Catherine Ashmore

130 (Bottom): Catherine Ashmore

131 (Top): Catherine Ashmore

132 (Bottom): Catherine Asmore

132 (Top): John Haynes (www.johnhaynesphotography.com)

132 (Bottom): John Haynes (www.johnhaynesphotography.com)

133 (Top left): Robert Day

133 (Top right): Robert Day

137: Malcolm Prince

138: Unknown

139 (Top): Unknown

139 (Bottom): Unknown

140: Unknown

141 (Top): Really Useful Theatre Group Ltd

142 (Top): Barry Plumber

142 (Bottom): Unknown

143 (Top): Unknown

143 (Bottom): Unknown

144 (Bottom): Unknown

145: Unknown

148: Michael Le Poer Trench